Reparenting

Reparenting

A Re-opportunity To Have A Happy Childhood

**A Workbook Using Biblical
Principles to Overcome
Childhood Deficits
Volume 2**

Dr. Larry Gilliam
Romana Russum and Angie Gillis, M.S.
Preface by Frank Minirth, M.D., PhD.

REDEMPTION
PRESS

Reparenting, Volume 2

Published by Redemption Press, PO Box 427, Enumclaw, WA 98022.

Print Edition

The author of this book has waived a portion of the publisher's recommended professional editing services. As such, any related errors found in this finished product are not the responsibility of the publisher.

Unless otherwise noted, all Scriptures are taken from the *Holy Bible, King James Version.*

Scripture references marked NIV® are taken from the *Holy Bible, New International Version®, NIV®.* Copyright © 1973, 1978, 1984 by Biblica, Inc.™ Used by permission of Zondervan. All rights reserved worldwide. www.zondervan.com

Scripture references marked nasb are taken from the *New American Standard Bible,* © 1960, 1963, 1968, 1971, 1972, 1973, 1975, 1977 by The Lockman Foundation. Used by permission.

ISBN 13: 978-1-63232-187-9

Library of Congress Catalog Card Number: 2012919401

Contents

Foreword

THERE ARE THREE things I would like for you, the reader, to keep in mind as you make your way through this workbook.

One is that the book is intended to be practical, conversational, and user friendly. To this end, we have taken some liberties at the expense of scholarship and tradition. We are OK with that if you are.

The second thing is that I have used this material and approach effectively for about thirty years in counseling and in seminars. I am not guessing, experimenting, or trying to prove anything about the content. God blesses it because it was His idea. It works, and it will work for you, if you stick with it, meet the conditions, and give it time.

Finally, the two-volume thing is not a bad idea. The first volume is sort of pre-op: it is necessary preparation that gets you ready for the heavier experience. The second volume walks you through the actual therapy, which can complete your reparenting.

My instructions are here simply to put them in writing and make them available. The rest is up to you.

—Dr. Larry Gilliam

Preface

WORKING THROUGH CHILDHOOD issues, moving from the past to the present, taking specific steps in a nurturing journey, and growing in Christ are premises of reparenting. With skill analogous to that of a virtuoso, Dr. Gilliam elucidates a myriad of exciting details of reparenting. Unfortunately, many Christian fathers do not know Ephesians 6:4, which says, "And you, fathers, do not provoke your children to wrath, but bring them up in the training and admonition of the Lord." Too often, a child will repeat a dysfunctional pattern. *Reparenting* offers tools to abate this pernicious pattern.

My gifted colleague uses a plethora of verses in his task of laying out the principles of reparenting. Consistent with this desire, I could not help but muse a bit on Isaiah 43:18–19a: "Do not remember the former things, nor consider the things of old. Behold, I will do a new thing." Just as God helped the Israelites of yesteryear with the concept of moving beyond the past, God can help us today. One caveat I offer: although this journey is too emotional for a few, for most the journey is refreshing and resplendent. The goal is to embrace Romans 8:15: "For you did not receive the spirit of bondage again to fear, but you received the Spirit of adoption by whom we cry out, 'Abba, Father.'"

Finally, as I read this book, I was reminded of Ockham's Razor of the fourteenth century, which stated that explanations should be kept as simple as possible. Dr. Gilliam has done an exemplary job of taking an abstruse subject and making it both pellucid and pragmatic.

I previously recommended Dr. Gilliam's original book on reparenting in 2007. My recommendation has not abated! I recommend it even more highly today, now that Volume 2 carries the process of healing and recovery to its attainable conclusion.

—**Frank Minirth**, M.D., Ph.D.

Introduction

The What and Why of Reparenting

REPARENTING IS NOT the same as parenting; although, one's potential for effective parenting will probably be enhanced by it. It is not the same as family therapy; although, one's ability to maintain healthy, satisfying relationships with family members (or anyone else) will probably be improved as a result of the experience. Reparenting might be thought of as a re-opportunity to have a happy childhood.

Here is a little more sophisticated way of saying the same thing: reparenting is another opportunity for individual, adult believers to grow through and progress beyond certain personal deficits or limitations from childhood that may cause them to back into the future while focused on a painful past.

This is a good definition because deep inside you, there is a part of you that still thinks, feels, and reacts like you did as a child. That emotional child, wounded or healthy, will stay with you throughout your whole life, and it is that part of you which is the most sensitive to the pain you experienced earlier in your life. Whenever you get in touch with that emotional child, even today, you probably find that some of the pain is still as fresh as the day that it happened.

You see, time alone does not bring about healing to these kinds of wounds. There are actually steps and a process that you must go through to nurture and to heal the child within you. This process is called *reparenting*, and it includes the mentality that Christ described when He spoke of the need for us to become like a little child. Of course, He does not want us to be child*ish* after we have grown up, as it says in 1 Corinthians 13:11, but He does want us to become more child*like* in several ways, as He implies in Matthew 18:2–5 and 19:13–14.

Since no one had perfect parents and no one was a perfect child, all of us reached adulthood with certain deficits from our original upbringing—some greater than others. As adults, we cannot go back and demand that our parents somehow rewind our lives and correct everything that we feel should have been different. It *is* possible, however, even today, to tap three effective resources for the reparenting roles of nurturance, affirmation, and guidance that allow the vulnerable, little inner child to grow and experience healing. One resource is your adult self, the second is another caring person or support group, and the third is God Himself.

When you accept your personal role in allowing this to happen, tap the resources of another caring person, and apply the biblical principles, which allow God to fulfill the missing dimensions, your reparenting can be completed. You will then find that, in this regard, it is really "never too late to have a happy childhood"!

—**Dr. Larry Gilliam**

The V-I-T-A-L Format

I DO CONSIDER the format for reparenting to be vital. The approach, the strategy, the process, and the sequence all figure into the format, and to a large extent, they depend upon it.

As I recall, Alice in Wonderland once asked the Cheshire Cat which road she should take. The simple but profound reply was, "That depends a good deal upon where you want to get to."

Imagine a couple starting on a vacation, and the husband, who is to do the driving, asks his wife for a roadmap. "Which one?" she responds.

"It really doesn't matter," he replies, "Just grab one, and let's get started." *Not!*

Someone attempted to define the word *format* by noting that it is made up of the two smaller words, *form* and *at*. His conclusion was, "It must be some kind of *form* that helps you figure out where you're *at*!" Bingo. That will work.

> "Whether you end up as a placemat or a doormat,
> Can vitally depend upon your basic format."

Each chapter, therefore, has been purposefully designed to follow the pattern shown below, the initials of which appropriately spell the acrostic V-I-T-A-L.

VANTAGE POINT—This is defined in *Funk and Wagnall's New International Dictionary* as a strategic position affording perspective. That is a fancy way of saying, "Where am I, and how does the answer fit into the total picture?" This seems like a good way to start each chapter.

INPUT FROM DR. G.—This includes the basic material of the chapter. It may sound a little academic at times, but it is the information necessary for the next step or next point of progress.

TAKING IT PERSONALLY—This is your opportunity to mentally explore how the basic material relates to your unique situation. It is designed to be thought-provoking, to elicit insight, and to stimulate processing.

APPLICATION—This section takes on the flavor of a laboratory experience. It involves something to do. It includes action-type answers to the question, "So what?"

"LITTLE MONA DID IT!"—This is the ongoing true story of how "Little Mona" (severely and repeatedly abused as a child) and her adult counterpart Ramona struggled their way through each step described in this book. In this section, "Little Mona" looks back and beckons other wounded inner children to follow her footprints to healing and wholeness.

Chapter 11

Communicating and Interacting with "The Kid"

Vantage Point

SINCE THE VANTAGE Point is defined in *Funk and Wagnall's New International Dictionary* as a strategic position affording perspective, we should probably attempt, next, to determine where we are and express it in a logical and understandable way.

It is assumed that almost everyone who embarks upon Volume 2 of the reparenting journey will have already traveled through Volume 1 and that the footprints of that experience will lead you naturally from Chapter 10 of Volume 1 and deposit you gently on the threshold of Chapter 11 of Volume 2 with ease and continuity. (It is possible, of course, that for whatever reasons, some will start with Volume 2, just as some will at times eat their dessert first! It's OK).

A backward glance is certainly permissible, provided it is followed by a forward look. In other words, a brief glance over your shoulder can be helpful in gaining perspective if it is followed rather quickly by a refreshing, inspirational shift in focus to what lies ahead. Once again, you must avoid the temptation to back into the future while focused on a painful past.

Your backward glance should probably include a review of the Process Checklist as it was presented in Volume 1. It may be thought of as a roadmap or an overview of the journey you have begun. In particular, examine closely items 1 through 15. This will give you a reminder of the distance you probably traveled as you worked through Volume 1.

Take a few minutes right now to place a checkmark by each of the first fifteen items, if you feel that you have adequately completed that part of the process. If you cannot conscientiously check off all fifteen of the items, take the time to go back to Volume 1 and review the chapter that corresponds to the item you could not check off. This will be well worth your while, because the Process Checklist is cumulative, and the sequence of the items is significant. In other words, item sixteen includes the assumption that items 1 through 15 have been completed.

Process Checklist

___ 1. Pick up the workbook (Volume 1); read the introductory pages.

___ 2. Get started with a ready, willing heart (Chapter #1).

___ 3. Define and accept the concept of reparenting (Chapter #2).

___ 4. Understand and accept the model of the inner child as a legitimate, effective way of representing that part of you that still thinks, feels, and reacts like a child (Chapter #3).

___ 5. Learn how the child "shows up" and expresses itself (Chapter #4).

___ 6. Realize that some people have hidden (or locked) the child away deeply in their emotional basement and have a hard time believing that it exists at all (Chapter #4).

___ 7. Get ready to meet "The Kid" (Chapter #5).

___ 8. Get in touch with the adult's attitude toward the child (Chapter #5).

___ 9. Meet and greet "The Kid" (Chapter #6).

___ 10. Differentiate between the inner child and the outer adult (Chapter #7).

___ 11. Learn the Biblical concepts of *childishness vs. childlikeness* (Chapter #8).

___ 12. Accept the goal of becoming more *childlike* and less *childish* (Chapter #8).

___ 13. Learn more about your inner child (Chapter #9).

___ 14. Feel some feelings that might represent your inner child (Chapter #10).

___ 15. Try to understand how the child feels and why he/she feels that way. Get in touch with the emotions of the child (Chapter #10).

___ 16. Communicate with, interact with, and pray for this child (Chapter #11).

___ 17. Re-check the level of your attitude toward the child on the *G-Scale Hierarchy of Importance.* Design a strategy to raise your attitude toward the child to a higher level on this scale (Chapter #12).

___ 18. Assure the child of its safety and your commitment. Plan to do something that the child would enjoy (Chapter #12).

___ 19. Learn other ways in which you (the adult) can communicate with your inner child (Chapter #13).

___ 20. Learn some reasons why you (the adult) must communicate with your inner child (Chapter #13).

___ 21. Identify negative messages said to or by the child (Chapter #14).

___ 22. Replace the negative messages with positive messages (Chapter #14).

___ 23. Use music to reinforce the positive messages (Chapter #14).

___ 24. Explore what it would mean for you (the adult) to "manage" or parent your inner child (Chapter #15).

___ 25. Design an ongoing strategy for "managing" or parenting your inner child (Chapter #15).

___ 26. Improve your relationship skills and apply them to your inner child, including consideration of temperament and personality factors (Chapter #16).

___ 27. Complete your (the adult's) part in the process of reparenting (Chapter #17).

___ 28. Plan and allow for the role that "Other People" must play in completing your process of reparenting (Chapter #18).

___ 29. Plan and allow for the role that "God, your Father" must play in completing your process of reparenting (Chapter #19).

___ 30. Prepare a program of maintenance and follow-up to retain and reinforce the benefits of your reparenting (Chapter #20).

Repeating Your Vows

A couple's fiftieth wedding anniversary represents quite an outstanding achievement and usually is celebrated in a special way. Often the celebration includes an opportunity for the couple to repeat their wedding vows at their church or in the presence of a few friends or family members.

This is not done because the marriage contract would expire if not renewed. It is done instead as a symbol of continuing commitment. The gesture seems to say, "Even knowing everything I know now, after fifty years of marriage, I am glad I did it and would do it all over again." As far as I know, no one has ever responded, "No, I won't," during such a ceremony.

You will now have a similar opportunity to repeat your vows—the vows of the Contract-Covenant you committed to in Volume 1. It is not because the first one has expired. Like the fiftieth anniversary, it is more of a symbolic act that re-affirms your commitment to yourself and God, now that you understand a lot more about what it means. It is a good thing to do, and this is a good time to do it.

There is an old story about a man who started to swim across a lake. In the story, he swam half the way across and came to the conclusion that he could not make it, so he turned around and swam back to where he started. Obviously, for the same amount of effort, he could have completed the task.

You are now halfway through the process of reparenting. It would be wise to complete that journey.

Once again, please read and initial each of the numbered items of the Contract-Covenant that follows:

CONTRACT-COVENANT

1. I acknowledge that deep inside me there is a part of me that still thinks, feels, and sometimes reacts like a child. _____*(Initial.)*

2. I understand that this emotional child, wounded or healthy, is a part of who I am and will stay with me throughout my life. _____*(Initial.)*

3. I understand that time alone does not bring about healing and restoration to this part of me, but that there are steps and a process that I must go through. _____*(Initial.)*

4. I accept the idea that the nurturing steps of reparenting can be experienced and that God Himself can fulfill the missing dimensions and complete my reparenting. _____*(Initial.)*

5. I recognize my responsibility to myself (the adult); my little, inner child; the people I care about; and God Himself to work through the steps and process of reparenting. _____*(Initial.)*

6. I know it will not be easy, but I (the adult) do hereby accept this responsibility and commit to work through the steps and complete the process as directed. _____*(Initial.)*

Next, sign your name on the line below, where it requests "Signature of Adult," and write the date in the designated blank.

Then, put your pen in your non-dominant hand (the hand you do not usually write with). Read the inner child's promise to help. Then, use your non-dominant hand to print the name you were actually called as a child (first name only) on the line where it requests "Signature of Inner Child (Print using opposite hand)." Finally, print the date in the designated blank.

_____   _____
       Signature of Adult   *Date*

I promise to help.

_____   _____
      Signature of Inner Child   *Date*
    (Print using opposite hand)

There is one additional point of review that would be helpful before concluding this section. It is an excerpt from Chapter 7 of Volume 1.

I will repeat it here, word-for-word, so that you can continue moving forward in Volume 2. Fasten your seat belt. Here we go!

> You may be familiar with the "super heroes" called the Power Rangers. (My grandson used to keep me updated on things like this). In the T.V. series they would at times combine all of their super powers to form a gigantic robotic-looking fighting machine called a megazord. It could accomplish mighty feats and overpower monstrous evil opponents. It was also pretty awesome in appearance. But if you could zoom in and look in through its goggles (or its eyes), you would see all of the Power Rangers seated inside its head, operating the controls.
>
> At times it seemed that the big machine was being driven by a committee! At other times, one or another of the Rangers would take over and direct the total organism through a crisis or threat.
>
> In like manner, if you could take a look "inside your head," you would see a team of potential drivers. One would be you the adult. Another would be your inner child. Each of you would have access to some controls, but there would be only one steering wheel. That would represent your will, or in this case, your "steering will."
>
> At times the adult and the child will negotiate and agree on who is going to drive the organism. On other occasions, however, one or the other will rise up, take charge, and direct the person through a crisis or threat. On still other occasions, the two may struggle for control, and the person may behave randomly, irrationally, or may shut down completely and become immobilized.
>
> Here are a few tips to help you recognize whether it is the adult or the inner child who has taken control and has begun to drive the organism:
>
> 1. Emotional reactions (especially over-reactions) are usually the work of the inner child.
> 2. Serious, analytical thinking is nearly always the work of the adult.
> 3. Behavior resulting from the desire for immediate gratification usually originates with the inner child. (The Kid can't wait!)
> 4. Behavior resulting from delayed gratification is nearly always the work of the adult. (The adult can decide to wait.)
> 5. The inner child is often creative, curious, playful, and spontaneous.
> 6. The adult is often logical, predictable, formal, and inhibited according to rules or regulations.
> 7. In general, the inner child exhibits childish and immature attitudes and behaviors.
> 8. In general, the adult exhibits more grown up and mature attitudes and behaviors.
> 9. At times the child may surface, and an adult may behave in a delightful childlike manner. This is good and healthy, unless it is excessive or at inappropriate times.
> 10. At other times the child may surface, and an adult may behave in a socially unacceptable childish manner. This is usually undesirable and unhealthy, but it happens very often.

Input from Dr. G.

Please notice that the title of this chapter is "Communicating and Interacting with 'The Kid.'" More specifically, notice that item sixteen on the Process Checklist says, "Communicate with, interact with, and pray for this child." Obviously, this chapter will focus on the necessity for and the importance of effective, two-way exchanges between your adult and your inner child in the process of reparenting. Attention will also be given to some methods through which this may be done.

The question is, "How can I, the adult, communicate and interact with my inner child?" The first part of the answer is that it already happens frequently, even if you are not consciously aware of it. The second part of the answer is that you can become better and better at detecting and defining when it is happening. The third part of the answer is that you can do this on purpose and with purpose by using the techniques described in this section. Notice that the following items form an acrostic that spells COMMUNICATE.

Some Methods of Communicating with the Inner Child

Childlike activities (participating as an adult)

Opposite hand-written conversation

Music (listening, singing, composing)

Metaphors (stories), meditation, and prayer

Unmasking (safely and wisely)

Nurturing children, pets, teddy bears, etc.

Interpreting/decoding certain dreams

Creative expression

Allowing the positive input of certain adults to revise some old, negative, internal messages

Taking part in group exercises designed to enhance integration between the child and adult

Empty chair exercise, examining photos, and emotional markers

Don't be concerned if the methods on the previous page don't seem to make sense. I simply listed them first as an acrostic in order to give the reader an overview. Now we'll take the items one at a time and explain what they mean and how they look when you do them.

Childlike activities: This simply means to participate in some activities that children often like to do. It could involve playing certain games, going to a playground, buying yourself a toy, or any number of other types of activities. Watching children at an elementary school at play during recess can give you some ideas. Your participation as an adult will likely bring some surprising emotions to the surface.

Opposite hand-written conversation: The adult can write a question or a comment. Then, the pen or pencil can be shifted to the other hand (the one not usually used for writing), and the child can respond. The response often resembles the handwriting of a child. Often, the child may actually respond with a meaningful or significant insight.

Music (listening, singing, composing): Music has been called the "universal language." It is well known that certain types of music bring out certain types of feelings or emotions. Simply listening to selected music can sometimes cause the child part of you to surface. Singing or otherwise participating in children's songs can enhance communication with the inner child. The inner child may especially delight in being allowed to improvise, compose, or express itself creatively in or through music.

Metaphors (stories), meditation, and prayer: This letter *M* stands first for metaphors. These are stories designed to produce visual images through which a person can feel safe and relaxed so that he or she may be open to allowing further exploration of feelings. In other words, these types of stories are not just for interest or analogy but will often touch deeply hidden emotions. A small child has an amazing ability to relate to a character in a story who is experiencing something with which he, the child, is familiar. *M* also stands for meditation, which, in this case, means prayerful consideration of situations, circumstances, certain memories, and potential solutions.

Unmasking (safely and wisely): Behind the many masks that you may wear is the precious, little person we call the *inner child*. In order for this little person to receive healing and restoration, certain protective masks must be removed in a manner that is gentle, safe, and wise. In the process of reparenting, some exercises are designed for this purpose.

Nurturing children, pets, teddy bears, etc.: Children like to nurture small animals, teddy bears, etc. because they need the nurturing themselves. When an adult nurtures children, pets, and so forth, the child within gets a special kind of benefit that he\she might have missed earlier in life.

Interpreting/decoding certain dreams: Dreams are sometimes an attempt of one part of you (at the subconscious level) to communicate with another part of you (at the conscious level). The message, however, is often in code or wearing a disguise. Decoding and interpreting these kinds of dreams can be extremely helpful and insightful in the process of reparenting.

Creative expression: Arts, crafts, and hobbies provide great opportunities for the inner child to surface and express itself, especially when there is freedom to be truly creative. In fact, such activities can be initiated by the adult to encourage participation by the child.

Allowing the positive input of certain adults to revise some old, negative, internal messages: People tend to act out the negative messages they learn in childhood. In an atmosphere of safety and acceptance, certain exercises can be effective in identifying and replacing old, negative, internal messages.

Taking part in group exercises designed to enhance integration between child and adult: It is necessary to tap three effective resources to foster the healthy integration of the inner child and the adult. One resource is your adult self, the second is another caring person or support group, and the third is God Himself. On a daily basis, the people whom we admire and trust are influencing us in certain ways, whether we are aware of it or not. The positive impact of these other people, however, may be enhanced and accelerated by participating in appropriate group exercises designed for that purpose.

Empty chair exercise, examining photos, and emotional markers: These three activities have something in common; they all stimulate the use of the imagination to get in touch with feelings that represent the inner child. Whether we are imagining the little person in the empty chair, trying to recall the thoughts and feelings of the little person in a photo, or designing an experience to emotionally mark a point of progress, something abstract should appear on the monitor of the mind's eye that can result in a positive change or a healthy shift during the process of reparenting.

Taking It Personally

In this chapter, "Taking It Personally" is designed to be a mental exercise with some emotional effects. The next section ("Application") will be more experiential and activity-oriented, but for now, get your "thinking cap" on!

Look back over the Methods of Communicating with the Inner Child, which you have just finished reading. Take the methods one at a time, and try to imagine how each would look and feel if you actually did it now, as an adult.

For example, begin with "Childlike Activities." Select a specific activity that children often like to do, and imagine yourself doing it. In your mind, make the decisions you would have to make if you were physically participating, such as, where you would do it, who you would do it with, and what equipment or attire you would need. Now, as vividly as possible, imagine yourself doing the activity. See the action happening in your mind's eye. Next, imagine how you might feel during and after the activity. Then, respond to the questions below:

NOTE: Just as "Little Debbie" (the inner child of Deborah Freeman) walked with you through each chapter of Volume 1, "Little Mona", (the inner child of Ramona Russum) will do the same for you in Volume 2. In both cases, they successfully walked the journey before you and, therefore, can offer some guidance, some empathy, and some encouraging words along the way. For example, in the following exercises, we are letting you know how Ramona responded to some of the questions. Your answers do not need to be like hers.

1. **Childlike Activities**

   a. What specific activity did you select to think about? (Mona put, "I chose to think about playing with dolls.")

   _____

   _____

   _____

   _____

   b. What specific decisions, choices, or assumptions did you make in the process? (Mona put, "I would feel awkward, assuming that I was doing it wrong.")

   _____

   _____

   _____

   _____

   c. Describe the experience as you imagined it happening. (Mona put, "I would have this doll and be playing house. I would pretend to be grocery shopping and cooking. Then I would stop and wonder if I was doing it right.")

   _____

   _____

   _____

   _____

d. What feelings or emotions did you experience during or after it? (Mona put, "I felt inadequate and somehow neglected.")

_____

_____

_____

_____

e. What attitudes, effects, or questions remain in your mind after doing this imaginary exercise? (One of the things Mona put was, "Am I still doing life wrong?")

_____

_____

_____

_____

Continue doing the mental exercises with each of the methods of communication listed below, and answer the questions that follow.

2. Opposite Hand-written Conversation.

Pick up a pen with the hand you usually use for writing. With the other hand, pick up a crayon. With the pen, write on the line below the name or nickname you were called as a child. Put a comma after it, and then write, "Are you there?"

Adult write: _____

Next, with the crayon in your non-dominant hand, print the child's response, "Yes, I am here."

Child's opposite hand response: _____

Next, using the pen again, write "How do you feel?"

Adult write: _____

Then, with the crayon, print in simple terms the way you are actually feeling right now.

Child's response: _____

Using the pen again, write, "I will listen to you and care how you feel."

Adult write: _____

Finally, choose one of the following responses and print it with the crayon:

1. "Thanks, I need that."   2. "I don't believe you."

Child's response: _____

This was only a brief sample of an opposite-hand writing exercise, but please answer the following questions about your experience.

a. What is something that impressed you, positively or negatively, about this exercise?

_____

_____

_____

_____

b. What feelings or emotions did you experience?

_____

_____

_____

_____

c. Look again at the child's final response (above). Does it look like it was printed by a child? Why do you suppose you selected that response?

_____

_____

_____

_____

d. What attitudes, effects, or questions remain in your mind after doing this exercise?

_____

_____

_____

_____

3. Music (listening, singing, composing)

a. Name two or three children's songs that you know. If you can't think of any, get someone to help you.

_____

_____

_____

_____

b. Which one of these songs is most likely to get in touch with the child within you? Why?

_____

_____

_____

_____

c. Write a few lines of a song that touches you emotionally as an adult.

_____

_____

_____

_____

d. If you had to make a choice to actually do one of the following, which would you select? (Check one.)

____ Listen to a children's song.

____ Sing a children's song.

____ Compose a children's song.

What does your choice tell you about yourself?

4. Metaphors (stories), meditation, and prayer

A little girl loved her daddy very much. Each evening when he came home from work, he would sit in a big chair by the fireplace. She would bring him his slippers and then jump up into his lap. He would say, "Do you love Daddy?"

She would answer, "Yes."

Then he would ask, "How much do you love Daddy?"

She would answer, "More than anything in the world!"

He would then give her a big smile and a big hug, and she would run and play.

One day Daddy bought her a tiny ring in a toy store. It didn't cost much, but she loved it because her Daddy gave it to her, and she wore it until it got old and turned sort of green.

Then one evening Daddy came home as usual. He sat in the big chair. She brought him his slippers, then jumped into his lap. He asked, "Do you love Daddy?"

She answered, "Yes."

He asked, "How much do you love Daddy?"

She answered, "More than anything else in the world."

Then he said, "Well, if you really love Daddy, give me your ring."

She giggled and replied, "Daddies don't wear rings like this!"

He said, "I know, but if you really love Daddy, give me your ring."

She took it off and, with a puzzled expression, placed it in his hand. He then tossed it into the fireplace, and a roaring fire consumed it.

He looked at her again and asked, "Do you still love Daddy?"
With a tear rolling down her cheek, she softly answered, "Yes, I still love Daddy."
"How much?" he asked.
She whispered, "More than anything else in the world."
"Then reach in Daddy's shirt pocket," he said as his big, familiar smile returned.
She reached into his shirt pocket and pulled out the most beautiful diamond ring she had ever seen.
As he placed it on her little finger, Daddy used that opportunity to teach her a wonderful truth. He referred to the Heavenly Father above, who loves her very much. He explained that at times when the Heavenly Father seems to take from us something we dearly love, He is then in the process of replacing an inexpensive toy ring with a beautiful diamond.
So tell Him you still love Him—and reach into his pocket....

Please meditate for a moment upon this metaphor. Then pray that God will apply its message to your heart. Finally, add the request that your little child within will become convinced that you have a Heavenly Daddy and that He is good all the time.

If you have a problem praying this prayer, discuss it here, talk to someone spiritual whom you can trust, or call a Dayspring counselor at 972-570-9828. (Dayspring Counseling Main Office is in Irving, Texas.)

_____

_____

5. Unmasking (safely and wisely)

It is neither safe nor wise to unmask in front of just anyone. A wise person once advised, "Only show your wounds to a healer." It is possible, however, to find a safe place and safe people who can guide you in getting to know the precious little person behind the masks.

One exercise that we use in seminars asks people to list several adult titles they may wear. Some of these might be job titles, parental titles, offices held (i.e., PTA President), skills you may have attained (i.e., guitar player), hobbies or recreational interests (i.e., golfer), and many others.

a. Please select seven or eight such adult titles that apply to you, and write them in the following space.

_____

_____

_____

_____

If we were in a seminar, I would ask you to copy these adult titles onto adhesive labels and actually stick them onto your shoulders and chest. Next, I would place an empty chair at the front of the room and ask you to imagine yourself sitting in that chair, dressed as you are, with all of the adult labels showing. Take a moment now, and imagine how that would look.

Now, in your mind's eye, begin to remove the adult labels, one at a time, thinking about what it would be like to give up each label or adult role. Remove first the one(s) that would be easiest for you to give up. Continue removing each label and thinking how life would be different without each of those roles. Save for last the ones that would actually be the hardest for you to surrender.

Finally, after all adult labels have been removed and discarded, think seriously about the person left in the chair. This remaining person is probably your inner child, unmasked and vulnerable.

b. Which labels were easy for you to remove and discard?

_____

_____

_____

_____

c. Which labels were the hardest for you to remove and discard? Why?

_____

_____

_____

_____

d. Describe the unmasked, vulnerable person left in the chair.

_____

_____

_____

_____

    e.   Discuss any feelings, attitudes, or surprises you experienced during or after this exercise.

_____

_____

_____

_____

6. Nurturing children, pets, teddy bears, etc.

    a.   When you think about holding a small child in your lap, how do you feel?

_____

_____

_____

_____

    b.   If you could choose any kind of cuddly pet to feed or to hold, what would you choose? Why?

_____

_____

_____

_____

c. As a child, did you ever have a stuffed animal or "blankie" you liked to hold or maybe sleep with? Yes or no? If yes, describe it.

_____

_____

_____

_____

d. Why do you suppose most people wanted or needed these things at some time in their lives?

_____

_____

_____

_____

7. **Interpreting/decoding certain dreams**

Can you recall a dream that you have had that probably had a hidden message, a theme, or some meaning that was in disguise or code? If so, discuss at least one example in which you can figure out the meaning behind the code or disguise in the dream. (If you can't do this with one of your own dreams, borrow an example from a friend or a relative. Most people have at some time learned something about themselves from a dream.)

_____

_____

_____

_____

8. Creative expression

Think about some arts, crafts, or hobbies that people sometimes enjoy. If you do not have much personal experience with these types of activities, you may need to call a friend for some input. Or you could actually visit a hobby shop or craft class. The purpose is to gain enough awareness of arts, crafts, or hobbies that you will be able to list eight to ten specific ways in which a person can express himself or herself creatively.

a. Please write such a list in the space that follows:

_____

_____

_____

_____

b. Now give some thought to which two or three of these activities would be most enjoyable for you. List them below.

_____

_____

_____

_____

The more freely and truly expressive the activity feels, the more likely you are to get in touch with your inner child. If you think that you understand this, write the word "yes" _____. If, however, this type of activity has absolutely no appeal to you, write "Not my thing!" and keep moving: _____.

9. Allowing the positive input of certain adults to revise some old, negative, internal messages

There were impressionable times in your life, when people who were important to you said things about you that you believed. Some of these things were positive, and some of them were negative. Some were true, and some were false. Some are still a part of your belief system and still affect your attitude towards yourself. Time alone will not change this. Some of these messages were not spoken but were transmitted by the way you were treated. Some examples of negative, internal messages are as follows:

"You can never do anything right."
"You will never amount to anything."
"You are not very likeable (or loveable)."
"You are not as smart or talented as others."
"You are not attractive."
"Having you was a mistake."/"You were a mistake."
"Whatever you do will not be good enough."

a. What are a few negative, internal messages that you believe (or used to believe) about yourself?

_____

_____

_____

_____

b. Who may have originally caused you to believe these things about yourself?

_____

_____

_____

_____

c. List some positive statements that are worded in such a way that they counteract or contradict those negative beliefs.

_____

_____

_____

_____

d. Who would you like to hear say and mean these positive things?

_____

_____

_____

_____

At this point in our reparenting seminar, we often invite six or seven volunteers to participate in a rather intense exercise. With appropriate instrumental music playing in the background, we blindfold the volunteers and seat them in a circle of chairs. Other seminar participants are then selected to take the worksheets on which the volunteers wrote positive words and sentences they would like to hear and from whom they would like to hear them. Using these sheets, the selected participants go around behind the volunteers and whisper or speak softly the words they needed to hear until every volunteer has heard the desired words several times. The effect is often highly emotional and amazing. While the adult volunteer knows that the words are being spoken by other seminar participants, the inner child does not seem to realize this and often reacts on a deep, emotional level. Sometimes significant emotional healing occurs.

Look back at what you wrote earlier and who you said you would like to hear saying and meaning those things. Imagine how it might be to hear those things actually spoken in the setting and manner described above.

Write a sentence or two about it.

_____

_____

_____

_____

10. Taking part in group exercises designed to enhance integration between child and adult

The final portion of the previous exercise (number 9), which involved six or seven volunteers and some selected seminar participants, is a good example of a group exercise designed to enhance integration between child and adult. It not only initiates communication, but also it fosters a certain positive change in the relationship itself.

When we use the term *integration,* we are talking about a relationship that continues to get healthier and more appropriate. It needs to be clearly stated that the child is not going to disappear. The purpose of reparenting is not for the adult to consume The Kid! Both parts of you will remain throughout your life. It would be most accurate to think of it as a dynamic relationship that moves more and more toward the characteristics of mutual respect, effective communication, and loving parental management of the child by the adult.

This will sound strange to some readers because these characteristics do not correspond to your concept of good parenting. Maybe your idea of parenting needs to be "tweaked" before your idea of reparenting can be healthy. Let's give Erma Bombeck a shot at doing the tweaking:

Treat Friends, Kids the Same

On TV the other day, a leading child psychologist said parents should treat their children as they would treat their best friend ... with courtesy, dignity and diplomacy.

"I have never treated my children any other way," I told myself. But later that night, I thought about it. Did I really talk to my best friends like I talked to my children? Just suppose…our good friends, Fred and Eleanor, came to dinner one night and…

"Well, it's about time you two got here! What have you been doing? Dawdling? Leave those shoes outside, Fred. They've got mud on them. And shut the door. Were you born in a barn?

"So, Eleanor, how have you been? I've been meaning to have you over for such a long time. Fred! Take it easy on the chip dip or you'll ruin your dinner. I didn't work over a hot stove all day long to have you nibble like some bird.

"Heard from any of the gang lately? Got a card from the Martins. Yes, they're in Lauderdale again. They go every year to the same spot. What's the matter with you, Fred? You're fidgeting. Of course you have to go. It's down the hall, first door on the left. And I don't want to see a towel in the middle of the floor when you're finished.

"Did you wash your face before you came, Eleanor? I see a dark spot around your mouth. I guess it's a shadow. So, how're your children? If you ask me I think summer school is great for them. Is everybody hungry? Then, why don't we go in to dinner? You all wash up, and I'll take up the food. Don't tell me your hands are clean, Eleanor. I saw you playing with the dog.

"Fred, you sit over there and, Eleanor, you can sit with the half glass of milk. You know you're all elbows when it comes to milk. There now, your host will say grace.

"Fred, I don't see any cauliflower on your plate. Have you ever tried it? Well, try a spoonful. If you don't like it I won't make you finish it, but if you don't try it, you can just forget dessert. And sit up straight or your spine will grow that way. Now, what were we talking about? Oh yes, the Gerbers. They sold their house. I mean they took a beating, but ... Eleanor, don't talk with food in your mouth. I can't understand a word you're saying. And use your napkin."

At that moment in my fantasy, my son walked into the room. "How nice of you to come," I said pleasantly.

"Now what did I do," he sighed.

—Erma Bombeck

11. Empty chair exercise, examining photos, and emotional markers

Empty chair exercises are not new. An example of such an exercise was presented under number five in this section: "Unmasking (safely and wisely)." This type of exercise requires the use of imagination to produce thoughts and feelings for consideration and modification.

Old photos may be examined to recall and explore circumstances that may have been forgotten or hidden away in the recesses of one's mind. With guided attention to certain details, such photos can be meaningful resources for communication between child and adult.

Emotional markers may be defined as activities, rituals, items, or mementos that may be designed or adapted for the purpose of marking or memorializing a point of progress or the achievement of a goal in a manner that emotionally impacts the participant and serves as a permanent, positive reminder or symbol of the special occasion.

Emotional markers are especially helpful in the process of reparenting to mark segments of the journey to health and wholeness. In the Old Testament, piles of stones were often left behind to commemorate a victory, mark a covenant or set a boundary. In like manner, some emotional markers may be simple acknowledgements, such as writing a letter, painting a sign, or buying a toy. Others may be more complex or sophisticated, such as designing a special funeral service, ceremonially destroying a journal of personal notes, or gathering several people at a significant location to celebrate in a unique way.

Use the space that follows to show that you understand what an emotional marker is. First, as instructed below, describe an abusive childhood situation that someone may need to overcome. Then, design an experience that he or she may use later, as an adult in therapy, to mark the completion of a point of progress. Use your imagination. Be as simple or as creative as you wish.

a. Example of an abusive childhood situation that someone may need to overcome:

_____

_____

_____

_____

b. Example of an experience that he or she may use later to emotionally mark the completion of a point of progress:

_____

_____

_____

_____

c. How do you feel about the examples that you gave above?

_____

_____

_____

_____

Application

This segment of each chapter usually takes on the flavor of a laboratory experience. It often includes an action-type answer to the question, "So what?" In this case, however, there will be only one point to the application. In other words, the "So what?" regarding this chapter involves the need to be sure that you understand the crucial importance of communicating and interacting effectively with The Kid.

In one sense, it is impossible not to communicate something. Some type of interaction is occurring almost constantly between the adult and the child. The big question regarding communication is this: Does the message received equal the message intended? In the process of reparenting, it is absolutely necessary that the communication between the adult and the child be purposeful, pointed, and positive. Thus, the content of this chapter, including an understanding of the methods of communicating with the inner child, are of utmost importance.

To complete this section, use the acrostic that follows to list the methods of communication we have covered in this chapter.

Some Methods of Communicating with the Inner Child

C _____

O _____

M _____

M _____

U _____

N _____

I _____

C _____

A _____

T _____

E _____

Do you feel that you now have an understanding of each of these methods of communication?

If you answered *yes*, proceed to Chapter 12. If you answered *no*, review Chapter 11. Then discuss it with someone who might be of help, or call Dr. Gilliam or another counselor at Dayspring: (972) 570-9828.

Little Mona Did It

This Chapter 11 has been very difficult for me to do, mainly because of some attitudes and beliefs that I still hold onto.

I remember once, in an inpatient psychiatric setting, someone in a group said to me, "I'm glad you *are,* a girl." I didn't question my sexual orientation, but I remember thinking, *I am what I am.* I believed that boys were smarter, stronger, and more talented overall. My mother had that belief and shared it with me. The legalistic church I attended seemed to share those same views, so they were implanted deep inside me at an early age.

I developed a cynical attitude, like, "Men can get away with anything, but women better toe the line!" My personal experiences certainly seemed to reinforce that idea.

I cried during that group exercise that day. I didn't instantly get over my aversion to being a girl. When I saw pictures of me as a child, I did not like that little girl. In fact, I hated those pictures. Later, that changed a little, and I could look at those and say, "That's a cute little child!" as though I were talking about a neighbor. I was still disconnected, but I felt a little warmer toward her.

Then one day, after a lot of work and a lot of attempts to communicate, I looked at those pictures on the table, and I thought, "That is ME!" And I accepted her. Right now, I just want to say, "It was so worth the journey!"

One more thing about Chapter 11: In the exercise about "unmasking," the two adult roles that would be the hardest for me to give up would be "mother" and "writer." Those two roles are a major part of who I am, and I can't even imagine my life without either one of them!

Now, take a deep breath. Chapter 12 awaits!

Chapter 12

Improving the Adult's Attitude Toward the Child

Vantage Point

IN THIS CHAPTER, our goal is to assess and improve your (the adult's) attitude toward your inner child. A good starting point would be to define how we are using the word *attitude* and how it applies in this case.

We usually use the word *attitude* to refer to the feelings or emotions we have toward someone or something. Webster's *New Collegiate Dictionary* includes also the mental position we hold in regard to the person or thing. There are several other definitions listed, but there is one that seems especially helpful in making our task clear. It is the definition used in aviation, which is probably the most basic and distinctly literal definition. It refers to the position of an aircraft or spacecraft determined by the relationship of its axes and a reference point, such as the horizon or a particular star.

In everyday language, the attitude of an airplane refers to how well it is lined up with the land or water over which it is flying. When making a turn, for example, one wing tip will dip downward, and the attitude of the plane will shift until it straightens back up after the turn. There are some aerodynamic forces, however, that can deceive the pilot into thinking he is lined up with the horizon when he is not. There have been actual cases when the pilot believed he was appropriately lined up with the ground below him, when he was actually at a forty-five degree angle or even upside down!

You've probably heard the expression that someone was "flying by the seat of his pants." The seat of the pilot's pants cannot be trusted as a reliable gauge of a plane's attitude, because inertia can sometimes feel just like gravity to the posterior of the pilot! That's why instruments are necessary to avoid cracking up.

The same principle may be applied to the process of reparenting. Your present attitude toward your inner child may feel perfectly normal to you when it actually is significantly askew. It may feel normal because you are used to it, not because it is healthy.

This is not the time to be flying "by the seat of your pants." It is the time to use an appropriate instrument to determine how well your adult is aligned with your inner child. This will reveal corrections and adjustments that must be made in order to complete your reparenting. (It may also help you avoid "cracking up.")

Input From Dr. G.

In Volume 1, Chapter 5, we suggested that "***Input*** might stand for ***i***nformation, ***n***ecessary to ***p***rocess and ***u***nderstand the ***t***ask." In that chapter, we proceeded to introduce you to a simple assessment tool called "The G-Scale Hierarchy of Importance." This is the instrument referred to above, which is appropriate for determining your attitude (as an adult) toward yourself as a child ("the kid inside"). Here is the way it looks:

1.	Love	The best way to be important to someone
2.	(Mere) Respect	What you will settle for if you can't get #1
3.	(Mere) Acceptance	What you will settle for if you can't get #1 or 2
4.	(Mere) Attention	What you will settle for if you can't get #1, 2, or 3
5.	(Mere) Tolerance	What you will settle for if you can't get #1, 2, 3, or 4
6.	Rejection	What you will settle for/expect/seek out/require, if…
7.	Abandonment	What you will settle for/expect/seek out/require, if…

Examine the hierarchy above, and notice the descending order of the quality of the relationship as you move from number one to number seven. In other words, the highest quality and most satisfying relationship is one characterized by love. Respect is still high in quality and satisfaction, but it is something less than love. Acceptance is important and desirable, but it is of even less quality and satisfaction than love or respect. The other words continue to decline in quality and degree of satisfaction as they apply to relationships.

The word *mere* is included in items two through five for a reason. It is to emphasize the fact that each of those items represents *less* than love, ***and less*** than the quality listed above it in the hierarchy. For example, when you receive love, you also get respect, acceptance, attention, and tolerance. But when you receive *mere* respect, it may seem rather military and lack the positive, fervent affection of genuine love. For example, someone may instruct demandingly, "You don't have to love me or like me; but, by George, you're going to treat me with respect!" (Like, salute when that person walks by?)

Along the same lines, acceptance is good, and if you get respect, you also get acceptance. Acceptance can mean that we accept each other as human beings, with all of the rights and privileges appertaining thereto. Mere acceptance, however, can mean just that I give you your space and you give me my space, and neither of us wipes the other out—nothing more. Or it can be reduced to the kind of peaceful co-existence that characterizes the relationship between a farmer and his turkey… until Thanksgiving!

Furthermore, if you get acceptance, you will also get attention; but *mere* attention does not guarantee acceptance. It may mean no more than simply being the center of someone's focus for a time. It would be a mistake to assume that attention equals love, respect, or even acceptance. This error is often made by young girls who become sexually promiscuous or young boys who act out in the classroom; both are settling for *mere* attention and attempting to use it as a substitute for some quality higher on the list.

Next on the hierarchy is tolerance, which may be the best that some people hope for in a relationship. There is a book entitled *I Hate You, Don't Leave Me.* That title is describing someone who apparently has settled for *mere* tolerance and does not expect anything better. Is it possible that some people have an attitude towards relationships that says, "Just put up with me, and let me hang around. That's all I ask!"? The answer is, "Yes!" I have counseled several such people through the years.

Even more incredible is the idea that people would expect and settle for the bottom two items in the hierarchy, namely rejection and abandonment. I am sad to report that not only do many people settle for such qualities, but also they literally seek out people who will treat them that way and gravitate toward them. This is most likely to be the case with people who were treated that way by the people who were supposed to love them.

If parents or other people significant to them at impressionable times in their lives rejected or abandoned them, they are likely to somehow associate that kind of treatment with the love they really needed. In other words, what actually happened can somehow get crossed up in the psyche and get filed as what should have happened. This may be partially explained by the fact that we human beings tend to repeatedly seek out that which is familiar to us, even if it was (or still is) painful.

Taking It Personally

We will now use the scale to determine how you view and relate to your inner child. There is some type of relationship that already exists between those two parts of yourself, and the G-Scale will serve as a model to help you define or describe it. It will give you some nails to hang your thoughts on.

Please take a moment and pray. Ask God to help you realize which level on the G-Scale best represents your feelings and attitudes toward your inner child.

If you can't remember much at all about yourself as a child, or if you seem to experience little or no playful enjoyment as an adult, then you have likely abandoned your inner child emotionally. If this is the case, then circle *abandonment* on the G-scale below.

If, on the other hand, you sense emotions more closely related to anger, anxiety, or fear—or if you clearly dislike the child or all this talk about the child—you should likely circle *rejection* on the scale.

If you think of the child as rather pitiful and you feel either some sadness or some embarrassment when you think of the child, circle *tolerance* on the scale. This is also an appropriate selection if you feel some empathy for the child and understand that he or she probably did the best he or she could under the circumstances.

If you can imagine yourself as an adult delightfully doing something fun with your inner kid—or if you as an adult would really enjoy doing something playfully childlike with somebody's kid even today—then circle *attention* on the scale.

If your primary attitude toward yourself as a child is, "Give her some slack … she was a kid … she did pretty doggone well, considering," then circle *acceptance* on the scale. (Read the above quotation with the appropriate gender.)

If you are really pretty amazed that The Kid turned out as well as he or she did and you feel a warm inner glow of pride or admiration when you think about it, circle *respect*.

If you feel that you care for that child with the same unconditional loving favor that God does, you may circle *love* on the scale. But hold on a minute! This would have to mean that you feel total inner peace when you think about yourself as a child, that your eyes almost tear up with sympathetic affection when you hear touching songs about children, that you are mostly free of negative emotions as an adult, and that you buy a lot of Girl Scout cookies! In other words, almost no one gets to circle love at this point in the workbook. Sorry.

So, go ahead and circle the level on the scale below that best represents your present relationship with your inner child, according to the guidelines you just finished reading:

1. Love
2. (Mere) Respect
3. (Mere) Acceptance
4. (Mere) Attention
5. Tolerance
6. Rejection
7. Abandonment

Now, think about your selection for a few moments, and then explain how or why you picked that level. Was it very hard to decide? What were some of your thoughts as you were making your decision?

_____

_____

_____

_____

It is now time to make a clear-cut statement of your next task. To do this, look at the italicized sentence below. In the first blank, write the word you circled earlier on the G-scale to represent your present relationship with your inner child. In the second blank, write the word from the G-scale immediately above the word you circled. For example, if you circled _Tolerance_ (#5 on the G-scale), write that in the first blank, and write _Mere Attention_ (#4 on the G-scale) in the second blank.

Clear-cut Statement of My Next Task

"My next task is to improve my attitude toward my inner child by raising the level of my relationship with him or her from _____ to _____."

In order to accomplish this task, you will need to design a strategy that will utilize one or more of the methods of communication identified in Chapter 11. We will do this together.

Ideally, you will continue to improve your attitude toward your inner child until the level of your relationship eventually reaches the top level on the G-scale, which is _Love_.

Meanwhile, let it be OK for the level of that relationship to be wherever it actually is. After all, the only place you can start is where you really are. Resist the idea of focusing on where you wish you were or where you think you ought to be on the scale. Relax and inwardly agree to begin with the reality of where you are now in your attitude toward your little child within.

Initial the following statement to indicate your readiness and willingness to proceed: "I agree to begin with the reality of where I am in my attitude toward my child within, with the intention of improving that attitude by progressively raising the level on the G-scale until that relationship is characterized by love." _(Initial here.)_ _____

Application

You are now ready to consider the **ABC**s of achieving such an attitude shift.

**A**ccept the fact that it can be done. The first characteristic of a good goal is that it is attainable. Let's refer to Scripture for our assurance of this. In Colossians 3:2, we are instructed to "set our affection on things above ..."

The point for now is that we *can* set or re-set our affection. This is basically how we raise the level of a relationship on the G-scale. Re-setting affection shifts a person's attitude like re-setting a thermostat changes a room's temperature.

Be sure you understand the meaning of each level on the G-Scale. Think about each of them. Discuss them with someone. If you still have any doubts, check a dictionary definition. It may be helpful to review Chapter 5 of Volume 1, where more explanation is given.

There may be some question in your mind regarding the bottom two levels on the G-Scale, rejection and abandonment. Since the G-Scale is laid out in a descending order of quality of relationship, it assumes that being abandoned is worse than being rejected. The reasoning behind this position is that to continue to reject someone requires you to continue to think about him or her and to invest energy in saying or doing things to express that rejection. Even if you were to hit someone, your behavior would show that the person is significant or important enough to you in some way that you address, focus on, and invest the time and energy that it takes to strike him or her. In such a case, you would at least be acknowledging him or her as a person, although in a negative way.

On the other hand, when you abandon someone, you are no longer addressing or investing energy in that person. You have forsaken and ceased to acknowledge him or her as a human being. The message is that person is no longer significant to you, not even important enough to scream at, hit, or otherwise make contact with. That is why *abandonment* is at the bottom of the G-Scale Hierarchy of Importance.

As you may recall from Volume 1, Deborah Freeman had emotionally *abandoned* "Little Debbie" and had to start at the bottom of the G-Scale. It was necessary, therefore, for her to get in touch with and express the negative attitude of *rejection* toward the child in order to move to the next level. At first, it is hard to believe that this could be a good thing, much less a point of progress. It is progress, however, in the sense that the relationship moved from no acknowledgement to some significance, even though it was negative.

If you also have to start at the bottom of the G-Scale, use the following space to express your negative attitude of *rejection* toward your inner child. Own up to it (or down to it!), and do your best to describe it clearly and accurately in two or three sentences. If you do not need to start that low on the Scale, skip to the next paragraph.

If you need to start instead at the level of *tolerance,* then read the sentence below, and commit to what it says. Indicate your commitment by writing your name and the date in the blanks. If you do not need to start this low on the Scale, skip the commitment, and go to the next paragraph.

"I commit to *tolerate* my inner child, even when I don't like that part of myself very much. With God's help I will show patience toward The Kid, just as I would if I had to babysit a small child whom I could not spank, scream at, or hand off to someone else."

Signature _____ Date _____

Continue to improve your relationship with your inner child by continuing to work your way up the G-Scale. Target next the level labeled *Mere Attention,* even if you believe that you are already past that level. This exercise will give you a good running start toward your actual goal for this chapter, even if you are targeting a higher level.

Consider how important *attention* is to a small child. Remember situations when you have seen a small child begging for some adult to watch him or her do something. Children are constantly wanting someone to see or hear them demonstrate something they have learned to do. This need to have the undivided *attention* of some significant adult is so great that children will often settle for *negative attention* if they cannot get *positive attention.* Many times the child who is acting out or misbehaving in a school classroom is saying, in effect, "I can't get any *positive attention* in here; but *negative attention,* even punishment, is better than *no attention* at all."

The word *Mere* is included with the word *Attention* because at this level, no particular feeling is required on the part of the person paying *attention.* At this level, the only requirement is to provide the *attention* and give feedback that you are doing so. Your next assignment, therefore, is to design an experience in which you will be paying some *positive attention* to your inner child. The adult part of you doesn't really have to enjoy it, but The Kid part of you should have some fun.

Think about something you would have enjoyed as a child. Explore also what you might like to do if you were a child today. You may also get some ideas from the section of this chapter entitled "Little Mona Did It!" It doesn't really have to be sophisticated or expensive. You just have to spend some quality time paying some *undivided, positive attention* to your inner child. Include someone else's child also if you like AND if your "Kid" approves!

Use the following space to list some of your ideas. Then, explain in more detail what you actually decided to do.

_____

_____

_____

_____

Give the date and the approximate time of day (or night) that you did it.

_____

_____

_____

_____

Give a brief report on how it went. Include any observations, feelings, or after-thoughts that you experienced.

_____

_____

_____

_____

Which method(s) of communication from Chapter 11 did you utilize in this activity?

_____

_____

_____

_____

*Design an experience which will foster or demonstrate **acceptance** of your inner child.* Think about a few times when you really felt accepted by someone or a group. (Examples: "I feel/felt really accepted by a classmate when she gave me one of her bracelets to wear." "I feel/felt really accepted by two people at my new church when they invited me over for coffee.")

Describe two or three of these occasions by completing the following sentences:

"I feel/felt really accepted by _____ when _____

_____."

"I feel/felt really accepted by _____ when _____

_____."

"I feel/felt really accepted by _____ when _____

_____."

Use the information above to help you design your experience that will demonstrate *acceptance* of your inner child. For instance, if you can relate to the first example above (about being given a bracelet), then consider giving something to your inner child. (You may even want to wrap it, label it To/From, wait a day or so, open it, and play with it.) Or if you relate more to the coffee invitation, you may want to invite and take your inner child out for a shake, an old-fashioned soda, or some other refreshment you would have enjoyed as a child. If you need more help, go to someone who can help with some creative and imaginative ideas.

Describe below what you decided to do and why you chose that experience:

_____

_____

_____

_____

When you have completed this assignment, give the date and the approximate time that it was completed.

_____

_____

_____

_____

Give a brief report on how it went. Include any observations, feelings, or after-thoughts that you experienced.

_____

_____

_____

_____

Which method(s) of communication from Chapter 11 did you utilize in this activity?

_____

_____

_____

_____

Extend the same approach to the next level, for the purpose of fostering or demonstrating respect. Give some thought to times and occasions when you felt _really respected_. Consider what might cause you to feel genuinely respected even today. Share some of these situations by completing the following sentences:

"I feel/felt really respected by _____ when _____
_____."

"I feel/felt really respected by _____ when _____
_____."

"I would feel genuinely respected, even today, if _____
_____."

"I would feel genuinely respected, even today, if _____
_____."

Use the information above to help you design an experience in which you (the adult) would be demonstrating *respect* toward your inner child. Again, the adult does not necessarily have to enjoy it but must simply be willing to participate for the benefit of the reparenting process. Draw from your previous experience, when you demonstrated acceptance. Once again, if you need some help, it is acceptable to call on someone who can help generate some creative and imaginative ideas. The most effective helpers are those who enjoy and get along well with children and/or pets.

Describe below what you decided to do and why you chose that experience:

_____

_____

_____

_____

When you have completed this assignment, give the date and the approximate time that it was completed.

_____

_____

_____

_____

Give a brief report on how it went and who else you included (if anyone). Describe any observations, feelings, or after-thoughts that you experienced.

_____

_____

_____

_____

Which method(s) of communication from Chapter 11 did you utilize in this activity?

_____

_____

_____

_____

*Finally, attempt to raise your attitude toward your inner child to the highest level on the scale, which is **love**.* This means that you will eventually care about your child with the same unconditional loving favor that God does. It means that you will feel deep, inner peace when you think about yourself as a child and that your eyes will almost tear up with sympathetic affection when you hear touching songs about children. It means that you will probably develop a better sense of humor and be more or better able to enjoy playful, light-hearted activities, that you will be mostly free of negative emotions as an adult, and that you will probably buy a lot of Girl Scout Cookies.

To many of you, this kind of fervent affection toward your inner child may still seem impossible or highly improbable. Some of you may doubt that you can ever have this attitude toward anyone, much less that little child inside of you. The question "How?" may keep scrolling across the monitor of your mind. If so, I'm glad you asked. There is an answer to this question.

In Biblical terms, the answer is to set or reset your affection (Col. 3:2). The actual process may be summarized through the following acrostic:

Accept the Biblical truth that you *can* set or re-set your affection (Col. 3:1–2).

Focus on verses that clearly state that attitudes and feelings *can* change.

Find your feelings. (To whom or what are they presently attached?)

Evaluate. (Decide which emotional priorities need to be changed or re-set.)

Commit to set or re-set *("free up")* some of your emotional "hooks."

Transfer *"freed up"* emotional "hooks" to the inner child as "love energy."

Invest time, energy, and money to transfer emotions. (Use your will.)

Operate as though your affection has been successfully transferred (re-set).

Notice that your feelings (affection) will eventually come around, line up, follow, comply—i.e., Proverb 16:3—and *agape love* will be felt for the child. (Romans 5:5 reveals the dynamic through which *agape* becomes a reality).

Don't worry if this acrostic seems to raise more questions than it answers! It is a compacted overview of a six-hour seminar. For now, just fasten your seat belt, and keep moving forward! As someone said when the baby's diaper fell off, "The end is in sight!"

To get past the *A* of the acrostic, read the following sentence, decide to *accept* it as truth, and initial in the blank to indicate your willingness to continue working through the process.

"I accept as truth the biblical concept that I can set or re-set my affection, as stated in Colossians 3:2, and I commit to proceed through the process outlined in the acrostic above." *Initial* _____.

The first *F* in the acrostic requires that you *focus* on some verses that clearly state that affections, feelings, and heart attitudes *can* be changed for the better. As I was preparing for this chapter, I consulted my *Strong's Exhaustive Concordance* to locate a few of these verses. I was absolutely amazed at the large number of such Scriptures listed under *affection, heart,* and *love.* Some of those verses whose statements were clearest to me are presented here for your consideration:

- Romans 12:10 instructs Christians to become more kindly affectioned one to another/ toward each other.
- 1 Chronicles 29:3 tells how King David set his affection on the House of God, and the result was his sacrificial giving of materials to build Solomon's temple.
- 2 Corinthians 7:15 states that the inward affection of Titus changed, that it became more abundant toward the Christians in Corinth.
- Several Proverbs talk about changing heart attitudes by applying the heart unto knowledge (22:12), correcting faulty thinking (23:7), and by guiding your heart in the right way (23:19).
- Proverbs 16:9 reveals that a man's heart actually devises (maps out) his way.
- In Ecclesiastes, the writer communed with his own heart to make changes (1:16), claimed to have made his heart better through appropriate grieving (7:3), and finally was "cheered up" by his own heart (11:9).
- Jeremiah 3:10 reveals that it is possible to turn to God (or to someone else) with your whole heart.
- Ezekiel 28:2 reveals that the king of Tyrus "set his heart" to consider himself "as God." (This was *not* good!)
- In Ezekiel 40:4, Ezekiel was commanded to "set his heart" on all that he was shown. (This *was* good!)

- In Daniel 6:14, the king "set his heart" on Daniel to deliver him.
- Malachi 4:6 speaks of turning the hearts of fathers and children toward each other.
- Matthew 6:21 reveals that where your treasure is, there will your heart be also.
- Matthew 22:37; Mark 12:30; and Luke 12:34 say, "Love… with all your heart."
- Acts 11:23 associates one's purpose with one's heart.
- 2 Corinthians 3:3 speaks of things being "written on the tables of your heart."
- Ephesians 6:6 speaks of "doing the will of God from the heart."
- 1 Peter 1:22 instructs us to "love each other with a pure heart."
- 1 Peter 3:4 refers to the "hidden man of the heart."

All of these verses and others re-enforce the fact that affection, feelings, and heart attitudes *can* be changed for the better.

The second *F* in the acrostic challenges you to *"find your feelings,"* i.e., to figure out to whom or what they are presently attached. You can do this by asking (and answering) the following two questions:

1. Among all the *people* that you know, which ones can make you feel "the gladdest, the maddest, or the saddest"? Notice that the people who can make you feel the "gladdest" are often the same ones who can make you feel the "maddest" or "the saddest." List five or six of those people in the space below. (You may refer to them by name, by initials, by title, or by their relationships to you.)

   Examples: My Boss   My ex-wife   Our new baby
                      My son, John   J.D.R.   Sarah

   _____

   _____

   _____

   _____

2. Among all of the *"things"* that make your life entertaining, interesting, satisfying, or bearable, which five or six would you miss the most if they were suddenly taken away? They could include something as simple as a favorite T.V. program, something as personal as a pet, something as demanding as your job, or even something you enjoy eating or drinking. If you have an addiction, an obsession, or a strong habit, those could certainly be included

as *"things"* to which you are emotionally attached and would therefore miss. Answer in the space below.

_____

_____

_____

_____

Considering all of the people and things you listed in both of the questions above, try to discern the ones to whom (or to which) you have the strongest emotional attachments. Another way of asking the same question is this: "Which ones would leave the deepest emotional holes or sense of emptiness in your life if they were suddenly taken away?" From all of the people and things you listed in both questions above, circle four or five that seem to have the strongest amounts of feeling attached. When you have finished, please answer the following questions:

Was this hard for you to do? Why or why not? What were some of your thoughts and feelings? Any surprises?

_____

_____

_____

_____

The *E* in the acrostic stands for *evaluate*. This means that you will examine the emotional priorities you have indicated above and determine whether or not some of them need to be changed or re-set. It is likely that you will be satisfied with some of your priorities as listed, but further prayer and consideration may result in some areas of dissatisfaction. In other words, you will probably become convinced that some of your emotional priorities need to be shifted or shuffled.

Ask yourself if some of the people or things are too important to you, while others may not be important enough. Ask yourself if some of them have too much power over you and whether the connection is healthy or unhealthy. Ask also if your amount of dependence is excessive or maybe even abusive. Consider whether some of your emotional priorities need to be shifted, shuffled, changed, or re-set. If so, which ones?

Use the space below to explore and discuss these questions:

_____

_____

_____

_____

The *C* in the acrostic stands for *commit*, and it represents your opportunity to *"free up"* some of your *"feelings hooks"* so that certain emotions (such as love) can be transferred to your inner child.

In order to understand this process, please think of all of your feelings (emotions) as being represented by ten little bungee cords with hooks on the ends of them. In your mind's eye, imagine these little "feelings hooks" attached to the different people or things you listed earlier. In this metaphor, you have only ten hooks to spread among everybody and everything to which you are emotionally attached! In other words, feelings that are presently attached to one person or thing are occupied and therefore are not available to be used or attached somewhere else.

Although this is only a model to help us understand the economy and mutual exclusiveness of emotional attachments, the concept is an accurate and profound representation that has helped many hundreds of people to transfer, re-attach, and manage their emotions in a healthy and functional manner.

Although we could become clinical and pedagogical at this point, that seems neither practical nor appropriate to the author. To accomplish our task at hand and complete our mission, you need only to accept and apply the metaphor of ten little bungee cords with feelings hooks, as described above, and we can be on our way. If you so agree, please sign and date below:

"I hereby agree and commit to continue our task at hand by accepting and applying the model of ten feelings hooks, as described above, as a metaphor for freeing up certain emotions for the purpose of transferring healthy, positive feelings and attitudes to my inner child."

Signature _____ Date _____

The *T* in the acrostic instructs you to *transfer* some *"freed up"* emotional hooks to your inner child as "love energy." We have already established that such a transfer is possible. Then you explored where (on whom and what) your emotional hooks are presently attached. Next, you evaluated the situation to determine what changes and adjustments might need to be made. Finally, we have introduced the idea that the process of transferring feelings hooks *"frees up"* emotion and makes it available to be attached to the inner child as *agape,* or the safest and most appropriate form of *"love energy."*

NOTE: I would not be surprised if about now, a little voice deep inside you is trying to shout something like this: "OK, OK, I get it! Can we please get on with the HOW?" I can also imagine a rather high-pitched cheer or chant starting to echo these words through the caverns of your soul: "Get on with the HOW, let's do it now! Let's get to it, how do we do it?" And so on…

With all due respect to "The Kid" …
    There's one more nail that must be driven
    Before that info can be given,
    But if you'll rap my little song,
    You'll know it won't take very long!

(So, rap it… tap it… and slap it…)
    I can tell how bad you want it NOW,
    But first there's one more seed to plow,
    And one more insight to endow,
    But I will make this solemn vow,
    On bended knee I'll humbly bow,
    And tell you all about "THE HOW"!
    So, cool it, Dude! Don't have a cow!

(Written by my inner adolescent, impersonating my inner child)

In other words, there is one more concept to cover, and then you will be ready to un-hook, re-distribute, transfer, and re-hook some emotional attachments, according to better priorities! And the idea of doing this by "putting some off, putting some on, and putting some away" came directly from Scripture, namely from Ephesians 4 and Colossians 3.

At the risk of sounding a little too theological for a moment or two, I am including the following paragraph. It is crucial that you grasp the firm biblical base upon which this approach is predicated.

More specifically, Ephesians 4:22 tells us to *put off* that which concerns our former manner of life, i.e. the old man, which is corrupt according to deceitful lusts. Verse 24 of the same chapter tells us to *put on* that which pertains to the new man, which is created after God in righteousness and true holiness. Finally, verse 25 says to *put away* lying and other practices that sabotage our relationships with other people. Verses 26 through 31 get very specific regarding such behaviors. Likewise, Colossians 3, verses 8 through 14, specifically address things that should be *put off* or *put on*. After reviewing these scriptures, you will be impressed with the importance of transferring some emotional attachments according to better priorities.

The next question is *HOW* to go about doing it—*HOW to get it to actually happen!*

(Yes, Kid, the time has finally come! So…"Ready, fire, aim! Or better still, aim before you fire!")

The *I* in the acrostic represents the simple but profound answer: *Invest time, energy, and money to transfer emotions.* In other words, you become emotionally attached to the people and things in which you invest your resources. Your money, your time, and your energy are three resources in your life through which you can make such investments. Examine how you spend your money, your time, and your energy, and you will discover to whom and to what you are emotionally attached. If you want to make changes in your emotional attachments, you simply have to make changes in where you spend your money, time, and energy. The Bible clearly states that where you put your treasure is where your heart will be also (Matthew 6:21 and Luke 12:34).

Often in counseling we find the need to stop here and process the information in the previous paragraph. Please take this opportunity to re-read that paragraph. Use the following space to summarize what you believe it is saying. Express in your own words the simple but profound answer to "how we can transfer emotions," according to the paragraph above:

_____

_____

_____

_____

I would like to give you an example and then ask you for one: *When I moved to the DFW area, I wanted to enjoy Texas Rangers Baseball, but I really didn't know much about the team or the players. So, I spent some money and time attending a few games and some energy learning some stats, standings, and stories about the players. In a few weeks, I was not only interested, but also I really cared who won!*

Now it's your turn. Is there a person, a cause, or a ministry to which you became emotionally attached after investing your personal resources in him/her/it? Please give an example or two.

_____

_____

_____

_____

Now give some prayerful thought (or thoughtful prayer) to some ways in which you (the adult) might invest some money, time, and energy in your own inner child. This is not hard to do, and The Kid will actually help you! So will a friend, someone who has already been through this workbook, a minister or counselor, and God Himself! Little Mona's comments at the end of this chapter may also be helpful. Discuss below. One, two, three ... GO!

_____

_____

_____

_____

A guy named Roger Miller once wrote a song entitled "You Can't Roller Skate in a Buffalo Herd." It wasn't exactly his masterpiece, but it had these challenging lines in the chorus:

All you gotta do is put your mind to it,
Knuckle down, buckle down—do it, do it, do it!

Please take this challenge personally, and get started putting some of your ideas into motion. It will be an investment that will draw interest for the rest of your life. Describe one of the ways you actually chose to invest money, time, and energy on behalf of your inner child. How did it go, and what was it like?

_____

_____

_____

_____

What will you change, stop doing, or stop spending in order to "free up" some money, time, or energy to invest in this crucial project?

_____

_____

_____

_____

The *O* in the acrostic tells you to *operate* as though your affection has been successfully set or re-set. This means to go ahead and begin to behave the way you would if your feelings were already lined up with your new set of priorities. This is necessary because it will take some time for your "feelings hooks" to make their transfer, even after you have begun to invest money, time, and energy in your new set of priorities. In the meantime (and some times are "meaner" than other times), you may have to use your will and determination in order to *do right*, even before it *feels right*. During this time, your emotions will likely vacillate back and forth, and you will not be able to trust your feelings or make your decisions on the basis of how you feel at the moment. This is sometimes hard for (1) people who are used to getting what they want when they want it and (2) those who believe that how they feel is who they are. In those cases, "the tail may try to wag the dog"!

There is, in fact, a period of time during the transition when you will have to behave in opposition to your feelings, as though your emotional hooks were already lined up with the way you want to feel. An example of this from Scripture is in 2 Peter 1, where we are given the process of making changes that eventually lead us to the ability to love genuinely as "partakers of His divine nature." That process starts with your basic faith as a believer and leads you through several levels or stages in order to get you to the point where you can love right. In other words, this process will produce in you the ability to receive and give *agape love* genuinely and appropriately, even to and from your inner child! (See also Romans 5:1–5.)

It would be great to read and study these steps as presented in 2 Peter 1:5–7 because, as it says in verse eight, "If these things be in you and abound, you will be neither barren [alone] nor unfruitful [in your relationships]...." Verse nine concludes the matter, however, with a warning: "For he who lacks these things will be short-sighted, blind, and think like an unbeliever."

This may be seen as the biblical endorsement of a period of time during transition when you will have to behave in opposition to your feelings, as though your emotional hooks are already lined up with the way you want to feel about your inner child. While a few people seem to be able to make the shift instantaneously, the large majority of us find it necessary to work our way through the steps and the process described above. So, fasten your seat belt … and the seat belt of the little person on the passenger's side.

Finally, the *N* in the acrostic is alerting you to *notice* something you cannot afford to overlook! *Notice* that if you meet the conditions and experience the process described above, your feelings (affection) will eventually come around, line up, follow, comply—i.e. Proverb 16:3 and Romans 5:5. *Agape love* will be felt; and your attitude toward your inner child will be successfully elevated to the top level of the G-Scale Hierarchy of Importance.

Little Mona Did It

There was a time about eight years ago that I thought I had to abandon Little Mona, just to survive. I was physically ill, anorexic, angry, bitter, and filled with guilt and shame. Then, several financial crises happened at once; and to top it all off, I was sexually betrayed by a minister! I called that my "year from hell," and I became so desperate and overwhelmed that I had to get some kind of relief!

Little Mona was already so wounded and frightened from earlier abuse that all of this was more than both of us could handle! So I wrote her a "good-bye letter" and set about to disconnect from her any way I could.

I had been rejected by several people that year, so I rejected her for having feelings and needs and wants. Sometimes I rejected her for just existing. Most of all, I rejected her because "she was me," and I did not like either of us! But, as I said, I meant to abandon her so that we both could survive.

All my life, I would take whatever people gave, if I couldn't get love, respect, acceptance, or attention. Most of the time, I settled for mere tolerance. I thought, "If you'll just tolerate me for a little while, you'll be gone soon anyway, so it really doesn't matter." I also just tolerated myself, but I was stuck with me, whether I liked it or not.

In counseling, Little Mona would sometimes draw pictures of someone telling her to leave or get lost. I also had this image in my head of someone throwing something at a dog and telling it to "Beat it!" Dr. Gilliam explained to me that that was my inner child's feeling of rejection. He asked me to do some things with her and for her; and he also asked me to bring some photos of Little Mona, if I could. I brought him one picture, and I was thinking, "Here she is. Take her away, and take care of her! Keep her safe and protect her, because I can't!" I took one last look at the picture, and I thought, "What an ugly stupid, evil child! No wonder she was abused!" Then I gave him the picture.

Dr. Gilliam looked at the picture. After a few seconds (that seemed like a few hours), he smiled. Then he said, "I know this little girl!"

I thought I was having a panic attack right in his office! I thought, *Oh, no! He's thinking the same thing I was thinking!* I felt sick at my stomach and wanted to leave the office.

But then he finished his sentence: "… and I like her!"

Did he really say, "I know this little girl, … and I like her?" Yes, he did, and I think that was one of those "Kodak Moments," when a ray of light shines through a negative and leaves a positive print. We still had a long way to go, but something was a little different and a little better. I think it may have been "hope."

Little by little, I began to admit that Little Mona might not be as ugly, stupid, and evil as I used to think. I still didn't think she was worthy of love, but I no longer thought she deserved to be abused. Eventually, I was able to admit that there may be some acceptable things about her and that there may really be someone who likes her. Then, one day I noticed that her photo looked a little better than it used to!

The more I began to like myself, the better my life seemed to get. I'll be honest, other people showed a lot of love to me before I could begin to love myself. A lot of people helped me, and some even provided some direly needed dental work. I thought, *If these people can love me through such a huge and expensive problem, maybe I can love me a little, too!*

Every day since then, I've learned to love myself, even when I fail. When I sin, I ask forgiveness from God and others. I'm not saying that I never relapse, but I don't stay in relapse for months anymore. After a relapse, I choose to do the next loving and healthy action, and I choose that one day at a time.

My new, healthy self-talk is this: Failure is not permanent unless I choose for it to be. Love is what is permanent, and I will take the security of the permanent! And I remind myself daily Who and what is my Source!

Chapter 13

Improving and Expanding Communication

Vantage Point

A COUPLE CAME to my office for marriage counseling. After introductions and some get-acquainted conversation, I asked what had prompted them to come for counseling. Almost in unison, they answered, "We do not communicate!"

While I understood what they meant, I surprised them by responding, "That's impossible!" One of them asked, "What's impossible?"

I answered, "It's impossible for you not to communicate. The question is whether you communicate what you mean to. In other words, does message intended equal message received?"

I used that opportunity to explain the impossibility of not communicating *something* to each other. Even when you say nothing, you are communicating *something*. I told them about one morning when I sat at a counter and ordered coffee. I then turned to say, "Good Morning," to the man seated next to me but found that he had turned his back to me and was reading the newspaper. He said nothing, but he had made a clearer (or louder) statement that he did not want to talk to me. So I didn't say, "Good Morning!"

I taught them that at least 53 percent of communication is non-verbal (body language) and that at least 38 percent of communication is voice tone or volume (how you say it). That leaves less than 10 percent for the content (what you are trying to say).

A client once challenged this by asking, "What if the building is on fire? Wouldn't the content of that message be more important than the body language or voice tone?"

I said, "Maybe so, but if the building really were on fire, your body language would probably reflect the emergency, and you probably would not softly inquire if it were a convenient time for me to consider evacuating. In other words, your message would become believable when the urgency of it was validated by your body language and voice tone."

Now let's apply this to you and your inner child, so you can see why this chapter is necessary and valuable.

First, please accept the idea of the impossibility of not communicating. The fact is that some message is almost constantly flowing either to or from your inner child. Second, realize that because this is continuous, it is impactful, and if it happens to be negative, it can work against or even cancel out some of the good things you have learned to do in relating healthily to your inner child.

Third, notice that this dialogue has become so natural and automatic for you that you probably will not even recognize when it is happening. It will probably seem to you like normal, regular thinking, unless someone calls it to your attention or points out the difference. Fourth, acknowledge that this two-way mindstream of interaction (called self-talk) is too significant a factor to ignore. It must be recognized, accessed, addressed, and managed in order for your process of reparenting to be successfully and permanently completed.

Fifth and finally, prepare to raise your communication skills to the next level—especially those skills that apply to your relationship with your inner child. Even if you are already using all you have learned in the first twelve chapters, your progress will be at risk unless you improve, expand, and fine-tune your communication skills to accommodate the category of interaction described above, as well as a few variations that are even less obvious. That is what this chapter is all about.

Input from Dr. G.

When I refer to the stream of communication that often flows to or from your inner child, I am talking about a category of interaction that can easily be overlooked. You may be aware that it has happened, but you might not have a clue that it has actually been a message to or from your inner child.

The simplest and most common example of this is your self-talk. As you may know, self-talk is a term used to refer to the almost constant dialogue that goes on between two different parts of yourself. This dialogue is usually going on internally, but it may also be expressed externally. I'm sure that you have noticed yourself or others sometimes speaking aloud to themselves, i.e., externally processing.

Not long ago, someone in counseling described an argument she had with herself. She said, "I finally told myself, 'That's it! You are not going to get your selfish way this time!'" I asked her who was having that argument. She said, "I guess I was arguing with myself. Maybe it was my spirit arguing with my flesh. Or maybe it was my adult arguing with my inner child."

Some other examples of the not-so-obvious types of interaction that may often contain unrecognized messages from your inner child are dreams, slips of the tongue, or songs you may find yourself humming or singing inadvertently or without consciously selecting that particular song.

Through the years, many of my clients have found the keys to unlock mysteries of their early lives by examining and decoding the themes of dreams. As we have pointed out before, the actual meanings of dreams are often wearing disguises placed on them by the inner child, probably to keep the dreams from being too scary, too shocking, or too "raw."

While we are not suggesting that all dreams contain messages from the inner child to the adult, we are definitely convinced that this is often the case. In fact, we have found that such messages can be of great value in reparenting, since they originate at the unconscious level and may contain clues, cues, and significant revelations.

In the Walt Disney movie *Cinderella,* there is a song that says, "A dream is a wish your heart makes, when you're fast asleep…" I would add that this may be true of a good or a pleasant dream. A bad or alarming dream, however, may more aptly require the following revision of the lyrics: "A bad dream is a fear your heart dreads, when you're fast asleep …"

Dreams that are not considered or examined may be compared to letters that are thrown away unopened—some of which may contain something valuable. Dreams, like letters, should be opened, read, and considered. Then you may dispose of them, if you choose.

Some dreams remain in our memories for years, sometimes for the rest of our lives. These may be compared to letters that we keep because of reasons that are personal to us. We will explore some of these possible reasons in the section that follows.

Slips of the tongue are also very interesting. Sometimes you may be surprised or even embarrassed by a word that comes out of your mouth, which is not the word that you consciously intended. Sometimes you can see the symbolic connection immediately. Other times, it's not so obvious, so you just laugh and wonder where it came from. It is important to ask yourself what it might mean if it is, in fact, a word from The Kid.

Once, about the time I was learning about these kinds of sudden intrusions, I was rehearsing a song with a quartet on a Sunday afternoon. The lyrics to one of the verses began like this:

My heart will sing when I pause to remember
A heartache here is but a stepping stone
Along a trail that's winding always upward,
This troubled world is not my final home.

For some reason, I sang a wrong word in the first line. Instead of the word *sing,* I sang "My heart will *bring* when I pause to remember …" So I stopped the other guys and said, "Let's see what my inner child might be trying to tell me. What will I bring if I will just pause to remember?" Then I glanced at the clock and realized that I barely had time to run home to get my wife and children and get back for the evening service. My inner child had kindly reminded me not to forget to bring my wife and kids!

On many occasions, I have become aware that I was humming, whistling, or singing a song that I must have inadvertently or unconsciously selected. The title or a line in the song has frequently had a meaning that came from below my conscious level. One rather humorous example (for which I am grateful) helped me pass a Bible test my freshman year at Baylor University. I couldn't remember at the moment who succeeded Moses as the leader of God's people. Then there suddenly came to my mind a melody I had learned in Sunday School as a child. I hummed it and then recalled the words: "Old Moses failed, did not obey, And so the Lord called Joshua ..." (pronounced *Josh-u-way* in that song). That was the answer! Little Larry had come to the rescue. What a team we make!

The examples above originated with The Kid and floated up into the conscious awareness of the adult. Now, let's explore some not-so-obvious ways in which we may reverse the direction of the flow as we initiate messages from the adult to the inner child.

Earlier we mentioned the client who realized that the adult part of herself was having an argument with the part of herself called the inner child. She acknowledged an awareness that a two-way conversation was going on. This shows that such self-talk may go both directions. This, of course, means that it can go either direction at any given moment. This is significant because it identifies self-talk as one of the ways in which messages may be sent from the adult to the inner child.

It is certainly possible for the adult to make parenting statements designed to manage the inner child. When that happens, it is best for it to happen with conscious awareness, on purpose, and according to good reparenting skills. Hateful voice tones and words of rejection (such as, "Shut up and go away!") are as inappropriate in reparenting as they are in parenting.

Since self-talk is happening most of the time anyway, it makes sense to give some thought to how it may be used positively and therapeutically. Attention should be given to improving the quality and effect of your self-talk. Some prayerful thought and consideration should go into selecting the best words or phrases to use when speaking to your inner child. Time should be spent actually composing and writing out better ways to express things to the child part of yourself. Then you may have to read aloud the new ways of saying things until you can memorize some of the phrases or form the habit of using some of the better wording. Remember that it is important for the message intended by the adult to equal the message received by the inner child. This applies to the emotional effect as well as the content.

Another way to initiate interaction with your inner child is to consciously select music that brings out the response you are seeking. Music is a major influence in your life, and with a little thought, you can identify songs that produce or revise certain attitudes or feelings in your inner child. Whether you sing the songs or listen to recordings, you can get the attention of The Kid and send a significant message. I do this purposefully in certain seminars and sometimes one-on-one in counseling. Later in this chapter, there will be some exercises designed to demonstrate this method.

The biblical basis for this effective resource is clear. In 1 Samuel 16:23, King Saul calls for David to play his harp to pull him through a state of depression. Ephesians 5:19 identifies music as a method of speaking to one's own heart. Colossians 3:16 instructs us to use appropriate music for teaching, admonishing, and ministering grace in our hearts. Music is apparently an effective way of writing something on the "tables of your heart" (2 Cor. 3:3). Job and Jeremiah also attest to the necessity of truth and wisdom being written in our inward parts, namely on our hearts (Job 38:36 and Jer. 31:33).

From the earliest recorded history, it is clear that music has been used in this way throughout the ages. Scripture actually reveals eight purposes for which God created music, but that is another book. For now, just accept the fact that music is a major resource for influential expression and communication, which can span cultures, nationalities, as well as any gaps between your adult and your inner child. Music is truly the universal language.

Actually, all eleven of the methods of communication presented in Chapter 11 have potential for being used skillfully in the process of reparenting. Most people, however, find that two or three of those methods come easily and naturally for them, while some of the other methods seem somewhat awkward and less suitable for them personally. Later in this chapter, you will have the opportunities (1) to identify a few of the methods that suit you the best and (2) to attempt to get really good at using them in your reparenting process.

Taking It Personally

The purpose of this chapter is to improve and expand communication between you (the adult) and your inner child. So far, we have pointed out the impossibility of not communicating *something*, even if it is not what you intended. We have emphasized that the continuous, two-way mindstream of interaction (called self-talk) is too significant a factor to ignore. We have hopefully increased your knowledge and awareness of three other not-so-obvious types of interaction—namely, dreams, slips of the tongue, and certain uses of music. Finally, we referred to the eleven methods of communication presented in Chapter 11 and promised to guide you in selecting two or three of these to fine-tune as you increase your communication skills.

Now, let's attempt to take each of our examples a little more personally. Prepare to be stretched a little beyond your usual way of viewing or thinking about the following rather common experiences:

1. **Dreams**

   Describe below one good or pleasant dream that you had as a child. If you cannot remember one you had as a child, try using a good or pleasant dream you had as an adult. If you cannot remember any good or pleasant dream at all, use the space below to try to guess why you cannot, even through most people can. Then skip the next three paragraphs.

   _____

   _____

   _____

   _____

   Explain how that dream might have been the expression of "a wish your heart" made, as the Disney song suggests.

   _____

   _____

   _____

   _____

   If this good or pleasant dream does contain some message from your inner child, what might it be? Discuss any codes, disguises, or symbols in the dream, and guess what they might represent. Use your imagination or get someone to help you explore some possible explanations. It is OK if your ideas about this seem a little far-fetched.

   _____

   _____

   _____

   _____

   See if you can remember any emotion or "felt sense" that you experienced either during the dream or immediately after waking up. If you can, then try to remember some actual life experience when you felt the same or a similar way. This technique will often help reveal the real-life situation or person to which the dream is connected.

Use the space below to describe any insights or possibilities that came to your mind. (If you could not remember any emotion during or immediately after the dream, try using the feeling you are experiencing now. What actual life experience can you remember that brought out the same or a similar emotion? Could there be some connection? Discuss this below.)

_____

_____

_____

_____

Now describe one bad or alarming dream that you had as a child. If you cannot remember one you had as a child, try using a bad or alarming dream you had as an adult. If you cannot remember any bad or alarming dreams at all, use the space below to try to guess why you cannot, even through most people can. Then skip the next three paragraphs.

_____

_____

_____

_____

Explain how that dream might have been the expression of "a fear your heart dreads," as Dr. Gilliam revised the Disney song to suggest.

_____

_____

_____

_____

If this bad or alarming dream does contain some message from your inner child, what might it be? Discuss any codes, disguises, or symbols in the dream and what they might represent. Use your imagination, or get someone to help you explore some possible explanations. It is OK if your ideas about this seem a little far-fetched.

_____

_____

_____

_____

See if you can remember any emotion or "felt sense" that you experienced either during the dream or immediately after waking up. If you can, then try to remember some actual life experience when you felt the same or a similar way. This technique will often help reveal the real-life situation or person to which the dream is connected.

Use the space below to describe any insights or possibilities that came to your mind. (If you could not remember any emotion during or immediately after the dream, try using the feeling you are experiencing now. What actual life experience can you remember that brought out the same or a similar emotion? Could there be some connection? Discuss this below.)

_____

_____

_____

_____

Is there a dream that you have had more than once? If not exactly the same, are there similar dreams that you have had, or are there dreams that seem to have similar themes? If so, describe and explain how those dreams might have contained a message from your inner child, informing or reminding you of some unfinished business or unresolved issue that is (or was) scary or painful to The Kid. If you cannot remember ever having the same or similar dream more than once, please state this in the space below.

_____

_____

_____

_____

2. Slips of the tongue

All of us have, at times, spoken a word or phrase other than what we intended, but usually we simply correct ourselves and keep talking. We often make no mental note of the error—unless, of course, the unintended words are amusing or embarrassing! In other words, most people do not know to stop and ask themselves the following questions: "Might this slip of the tongue be a message from my inner child? And if so, what might my inner child be trying to say to me?" Sometimes the answer can be amazingly interesting or insightful!

Let me give you an example from my own experience. One Sunday morning, when I was supposed to speak at a rather prominent church, several things had caused me to be running close on time. To make things worse, I got confused and stopped at the wrong church facility, several blocks from where I was supposed to be. By the time I got back in my car, found the right church, and entered the building, the service had already started. I was escorted to the platform, welcomed, and introduced. As I approached the pulpit, I was planning to say, "It is a pleasure and a privilege to be with you today." Instead, I said, "It is a pressure and a plivilege to be with you today." (My slip of the tongue was the truth. It _had_ been a pressure, but I did not intend to announce that to everyone!)

At one counseling center where I worked for several years, there was a day when the receptionist was very busy. She had a couple of calls on hold, and the phone kept ringing. I heard her answer one line and say, "Would you hold for a moment, please?" Then she answered another line and said, "Could you hold for me a moment, please?" When she got to the third line, her words ran together and came out like this: "Would you hold me for a moment, please?" (Is it possible that her inner child was frustrated and wanted to be held?)

True feelings or attitudes may sometimes slip out, such as with the fellow who attended a wedding where his ex-girlfriend married his best friend. At the reception, he announced in a loud voice, "It is kisstomery to cuss the bride!"

A politically incorrect slip of this sort could have rather severe consequences, such as with the peasant who meant to shout, "Let's all cheer the dear old queen!" It came out, "Let's all cheer the queer old dean!"

Then there was the fellow at a church social who was attempting to courteously introduce twin sisters who had a rather shady reputation. He stood and said, "We have two guests here who are sin twisters!"

Finally, let's consider the preacher who meant to close his sermon with the words, "The Lord is a loving Shepherd." Instead he said, "The Lord is a shoving leopard." Might this slip of the tongue have revealed his inner child's distorted image of God as an angry, violent being to be feared?

Describe below a slip of the tongue, i.e., a time when some word (or words) other than what you intended came out of your mouth. It doesn't matter whether it happened recently or when you were a child. Almost everyone can think of some occasion like this, whether it was spoken or sung. If you cannot think of an example that was spoken or sung, try to use a time when you wrote or typed a wrong word. (NOTE: I am not intending here to refer to any experience that you believe was prompted by the Holy Spirit, nor to any which you may attribute to demonic or satanic activity).

_____

_____

_____

_____

Give some thought to how that slip of the tongue might have contained a message from your inner child. Use the space below to explore possible reasons why your inner child may have substituted the unintended word(s). What might your inner child have been trying to say?

_____

_____

_____

_____

3. **Songs you may find yourself humming or singing**

Try to think of a time when you noticed that you were humming or singing some song inadvertently, without consciously deciding to do so. (If you cannot think of such a time, then start watching for one. It will probably happen before long.) Use the space below to describe the lyrics, title, or meaning of the song.

_____

_____

_____

_____

Again, assume that there is some explanation for this that involves your inner child. If this is the case, explore the possible meaning. Remember that your inner child is creative and sometimes uses humor, especially puns and double meanings. With this in mind, discuss what The Kid might want you to understand, remember, or think about. Use the space below to discuss some possibilities.

_____

_____

_____

_____

4. Self-Talk (including interaction with the inner child)

There are times when all of us talk to ourselves. Sometimes it is a simple conversation. Other times, it may become a heated argument as we try to make a difficult decision or come to some controversial conclusion. It is hard for us to analyze our own self talk, however, because it is so natural for us; we do it all the time. As someone once said about a romantic kiss, "It is hard to be a participant and an analyst at the same time!"

It is possible, however, for us to identify some of our more habitual dialogues: first because we have repeated them many times; second because we have likely heard ourselves speak some of them aloud at times; and third because certain other people have probably heard us speak some of them aloud and made us pay in some way!

Your assignment for now, therefore, is to identify one such dialogue from your repertoire, write it out as best you can, and then examine it to see which parts of the interaction might have originated with your inner child. You will have hundreds of examples from which to choose, but one common example might be the process of deciding whether or not to eat something fattening that you do not need and should not eat.

A similar scenario might be the process of resisting or giving in to impulsively buying something you want but cannot afford. You can easily think of far more serious points of conflict in which the child part of you has strongly wanted something bad or strongly resisted doing something good. The adult part of you probably tried first to reason with the child. The child likely countered with all the childish responses that have worked in the past. The adult part of you may have given in, or you may have used your will to firmly manage or parent your inner child.

In the space below, select one such dialogue from your experience, write out in detail the exchanges as though they were a script for a play, including the decision or conclusion the way it actually played itself out in some real-life situation.

Describe the real-life situation or scenario you have chosen:

_____

_____

_____

_____

Start the inner child's first statement with the words, "I want ...," "I don't want ...," or "May I ...?"

_____

_____

_____

_____

Inner child:

_____

_____

_____

Adult:

_____

_____

_____

_____

Inner child:

_____

_____

_____

_____

Adult:

_____

_____

_____

_____

Inner child:

_____

_____

_____

Adult:

_____

_____

_____

_____

Inner child:

_____

_____

_____

_____

Adult:

_____

_____

_____

_____

Decision or conclusion:

_____

_____

_____

_____

Describe your experience as you did this assignment. What was hard about it? What was interesting about it? Did you learn anything or gain any insights regarding self-talk that may include interaction with your inner child?

_____

_____

_____

_____

5. Two methods of communication from Chapter 11 (the two which come more easily or naturally for you)

In Chapter 11, the following acrostic was used to introduce eleven methods of communicating with the inner child. Please examine them to identify two of the methods that seem to come more easily or more naturally for you personally. Feel free to review the definitions of each method in Chapter 11, if it would be helpful to you.

Some Methods of Communicating with the Inner Child

Childlike activities (participating as an adult)

Opposite hand-written conversation

Music (listening, singing, composing)

Metaphors (stories), meditation, and prayer

Unmasking (safely and wisely)

Nurturing children, pets, teddy bears, etc.

Interpreting/decoding certain dreams

Creative expression

Allowing the positive input of certain adults to revise some old, negative, internal messages

Taking part in group exercises designed to enhance integration between child and adult

Empty chair exercise, examining photos, and emotional markers

After prayerful consideration, put a checkmark by two or three of the methods above that seem like they would be easier or more natural for you to actually use. (NOTE: Do not select music or interpretation of dreams for this exercise, since we have already included those in this chapter.)

Now look at the two or three you checked, and decide which one of them would actually be the most fun for you to do. List the one you would probably enjoy the most as number one below. List as number two the one that comes in second, according to its potential for your enjoyment. Accept these two methods as the ones from the acrostic that you will probably use most frequently and most effectively in your reparenting.

1. _____

2. _____

Ask yourself the question, "How can I improve my knowledge and my skill in using the two methods of communication listed above?" Of course, you can probably find some books on those methods. You may be able to find some Christian counselor who can help. You could call us directly at the Dayspring Center in Irving, Texas (972-258-0022 or 972-790-3700). For this exercise, however, I am asking you to try something on your own and see how it goes. Give some prayerful thought as to how you might design two specific activities that would give you some practice in each of the methods you listed. Use the following spaces to describe your two activities.

1. Plans for an activity related to the method listed as number 1 above:

   _____

   _____

   _____

   _____

2. Plans for an activity related to the method listed as number 2 above:

   _____

   _____

   _____

   _____

   Date of activity related to method number 1: _____
   How did it go, how did it feel, and what did you learn?

   _____

   _____

_____

_____

Date of activity related to method number 2: _____
How did it go, how did it feel, and what did you learn?

_____

_____

_____

_____

Application

So far in this chapter, the six methods of communication we have identified for expanding knowledge and improving skills are as follows (Please write your first and second selections from the acrostic in numbers 5 and 6 below.):

1. Dreams

2. Slips of the tongue

3. Music

4. Self-talk

5. _____ (your first selection from the acrostic).

6. _____ (your second selection from the acrostic).

Let's consider these methods for further application in reparenting.

1. Dreams

You can get better and better at discerning which dreams include a message from your inner child. Continue to examine good or pleasant dreams to reveal wishes from the heart of your inner child. Continue to examine bad or alarming dreams to reveal fears that your inner child dreads and is afraid may come to pass. Even dreams that seem silly or bizarre may contain codes and disguises that can unlock serious themes that might otherwise be too scary or "raw" to the inner child. You, better than anyone else, may be able to decode cues and clues from your own inner child. There is often an exciting "aha" moment when you suddenly discover or stumble onto a meaning because of a memory or association known only to you and your inner child. You may find yourself wanting to do a "high five" with The Kid!

There are many books rather easy to find that define a few of the somewhat universal interpretations of dream symbols. Some of these might be helpful, but it has been my experience that most dream codes from the inner child are personal and subjective and are most likely to come to light when you are alone or with someone you can trust, such as a close friend or a professional, Christian counselor who has proven to be trustworthy.

Look back at the good or pleasant dream you described earlier in this chapter. Review the responses you wrote about that dream. See if there are any new revelations or insights that you gain as you re-read and re-think what you wrote. Discuss these below, along with any thoughts, feelings, or memories you may experience as you re-read your previous responses.

_____

_____

_____

_____

Next, give The Kid some feedback, letting the child know that you understand some things about the dream. Let the child know that it is OK to speak to you in that way and that you will be watching for more information about the wishes and desires of his or her heart. Do this by writing a letter to the child. If you choose to include a question, let the child answer it by putting your writing instrument in your opposite (non-dominate) hand.

_____

_____

_____

_____

Finally, affirm the child by drawing a picture together to illustrate part of the dream. Do this by drawing part of the picture with your dominant hand and other parts of the picture with your opposite hand. Color it by taking turns in the same manner. Include childlike humor if you can. The Kid will love it!

_____

_____

_____

_____

What was it like to draw and color this picture together with your inner child? Discuss some of the thoughts, feelings, or general after-effects of that exercise. Feel free to include both positive and/or negative effects

_____

_____

_____

_____

Now look back at the bad or alarming dream you described earlier in this chapter. Review the responses you wrote about that dream. See if you gain any new revelations or insights as you re-read and re-think what you wrote. Discuss these below, along with any thoughts, feelings, or memories you may experience as you review your previous responses.

_____

_____

_____

_____

Next, give The Kid some feedback, letting the child know that you understand some things about the dream. Let the child know that it is OK to speak to you in that way and that you will be watching for more information about the things that are scary to him or her. Let the child know that there are some ways that you can help him or her feel less afraid and that you are willing to help in any way that you can. Do this by writing a letter to the child. If you choose to include a question, let the child answer it by putting your writing instrument in your opposite (non-dominant) hand.

_____

_____

_____

_____

Finally, affirm the child by drawing a picture together to illustrate a new, different, and positive ending to the dream! Use the original scenario, but make the picture show the dream ending in a way that is pleasant, re-assuring, maybe even humorous. In other words, be creative and make the dream turn out well! Do this by drawing part of the picture with your dominant hand and other parts of the picture with your opposite hand. Color it by taking turns in the same manner.

_____

_____

_____

_____

What was it like to draw and color this picture together with your inner child? Discuss some of the thoughts, feelings, or general after-effects of that exercise. Feel free to include both positive and/or negative effects.

_____

_____

_____

_____

You may remember another dream (or experience a new one) since we have sort of opened the door for The Kid to speak to you in that way. If so, describe it below, and attempt to interpret any messages it might contain from your inner child, using the approach and the information presented in this chapter.

_____

_____

_____

_____

Next, give The Kid some feedback, letting the child know that you understand some things about this additional dream. Let the child know that it is OK to continue speaking to you in that way and that you will be watching for more information. Let the child know that you are interested and willing to learn more about what matters to him or her. Do this by writing a letter to the child. If you choose to include a question, let the child answer it by putting your writing instrument in your opposite (non-dominant) hand.

_____

_____

_____

_____

Finally, affirm the child again by drawing a picture together to illustrate part of this additional dream. As before, do this by drawing part of the picture with your dominant hand and other parts of the picture with your opposite hand. Color it by taking turns in the same manner. Keep in mind that the purpose of this activity is primarily to improve and expand communication by doing something enjoyable together.

_____

_____

_____

_____

What was it like to draw and color this additional picture together with your inner child? Discuss some of the thoughts, feelings, or general after-effects of that exercise. Feel free to include both positive and negative effects.

_____

_____

_____

_____

2. **Slips of the tongue**

   You can get better and better at noticing your slips of the tongue and discerning when they include a message from your inner child. If there is any new insight, experience, or application to report regarding this method of communication, please use the following space for that purpose. If not, just save the space for future use. You will eventually have something new to report here.

   _____

   _____

   _____

   _____

3. **Songs you find yourself humming or singing**

   You will likely have to remind yourself in some way to begin noticing the times when you are humming or singing a song that you did not consciously choose or select. It would be good to ask the Lord, as well as someone else close to you, to call such occasions to your attention when they happen. Use checkmarks to indicate that you have completed or accomplished the following steps.

   _____   Step 1: I have asked the Lord in prayer to help me notice when I am humming or singing a song that I did not consciously select, especially when it contains a message from my inner child.

   _____   Step 2: I have asked someone else close to me to call it to my attention when they notice that I have begun to hum or sing a song spontaneously.

_____ Step 3: I have now experienced an actual occasion when I realized (or it was called to my attention) that I began to hum or sing a song spontaneously.

_____ Step 4: I followed up Step 3 by thoughtfully exploring whether or not the song might contain some communication from my inner child. (There is no need to report here what your thoughts or conclusions were.)

4. Self-talk (including interaction with the inner child)

The key to using this method of communication is to figure out a way to start noticing when it is happening. Once again, use checkmarks to indicate that you have completed or accomplished the following steps:

_____ Step 1: I have asked the Lord in prayer to help me notice when I am using self-talk to interact with my inner child, especially when it contains a message of significance.

_____ Step 2: I have asked someone else close to me to call it to my attention if and when they notice that I am having a conversation with myself.

_____ Step 3: I have now experienced an actual occasion when I realized (or it was called to my attention) that I was having a conversation with myself.

_____ Step 4: I followed up Step 3 by thoughtfully exploring whether or not my self-talk might contain some communication with my inner child. (There is no need to report here what your thoughts or conclusions were.)

Little Mona Did It

Of all the different ways in which a person can communicate with his or her inner child, the one that works best for me is music. I've tried all of the methods used in this workbook, and all of them worked in their own way; but some really seemed like "work"! Some of them did not come naturally and easily for me, and it seemed like I was having to try too hard to make them work. But music seems as natural and easy to me as breathing, and that's the major method I have chosen to improve and expand my communication with Little Mona.

Music has always been a major influence in my life, and it has played a big part in my healing and recovery. As I was growing up, I learned the old hymns and children's choruses at church. I also remember hearing a lot of gospel music and country music. My grandmother had a lot of recordings, and she would sing along as she cooked and worked around the house. My grandfather would listen to country music, when he could get a station out in the fringe area of Oklahoma, where we lived at the time. He loved the "Grand Ole Opry," and he had recordings and a big book with all the names and pictures of the stars. I had the book and the songs all memorized by the time I was seven, and I could sing every word right along with the artists. I had a toy microphone, and I would sing along and then imagine that all those people were clapping for me! Then I would bow and thank them profusely! I felt that I knew the singers well, and I would often pretend to be living in their world for awhile. I would feel that I had some friends who really understood. This kind of pretending helped me to survive on many occasions.

They sang about love and happiness; they sang about hurt, anger, betrayal, and loneliness. They sang about God and church and the victory we have in Jesus. Through their songs, I learned that I can put up with a lot down here on earth, because someday, "When the Morning Comes," "I'll Fly Away" to "A Land That Is Fairer Than Day" and that "I'll Understand It Better By and By"! Somehow, the child picked up on these messages and found hope.

Then there was the time, a few months after my mother died, when I was watching a DVD of *Hee Haw*. Dolly Parton was the guest star, and she sang, "I Will Always Love You." I was seriously crying before she finished the first two lines. After that song, she said, "In everyone's life, there is a special someone that we love more than anyone else. Sometimes we are lucky enough to be with them, and sometimes we are not. Yet, with them or without them, we will always love them." Then she started singing, "Even if I should stay, I would only be in your way …" It was like my mother was talking to me, helping me understand why she had to go, and reminding me that she still loves me as much as ever. Those songs on that occasion helped me and Little Mona to adjust to our loss.

Of course, I wanted to be a singer like that when I grew up. That turned out to be all dream and no talent! As a teenager, I told my mother I hoped someday to be on the Grand Ole Opry, and she said that I might someday make it as far as the audience! I had a lot of music in my heart and soul, and it sometimes came out really well in the shower, but I had to find a better way to express it.

In my despair, I sat down with a pen and some paper. I poured out my teenage anger; frustration; sadness; bitterness; disappointment; feelings of doom and gloom; deep, dark depression; and various expressions of excessive misery. It just kept pouring out, and it flowed on and on. It felt great to express it, to get it out, and to put it down on paper! It took on kind of a rhythm. Then I noticed that a lot of it rhymed. I was amazed! My poetry had all the makings of a country western song!

My poetry got better and better, and I got happier and happier! It didn't matter anymore whether anyone ever sang my poetry. My poetry became my musical voice, and I could sing to myself and to God all the music that was in my heart and soul. Now I understand Ephesians 5:19, where it says, "Speaking to yourselves in psalms and hymns and spiritual songs, singing and making melody in your heart to the Lord!"

I wish for you the same passion I have experienced with music, as you discover and practice the forms of communication that will best connect you and your inner child. I pray that you will not settle for less!

Chapter 14

Replacing Negative Messages
with Positive Messages

Vantage Point

THE PROCESS CHECKLIST shown in Chapter 11 expresses the goals of this chapter in the following manner:

- Item 21: Identify negative messages said to or by the child.
- Item 22: Replace the negative messages with positive messages.
- Item 23: Use music to reinforce positive messages.

Ramona likes to refer to this process as "The Three Rs"—but she is not talking about "reading, 'riting, and 'rithmetic"! She is referring to *recognizing, removing,* and *replacing* the negative messages. (Go, Girl!) That's what *she* did, and she will probably tell you more about it in her part of this chapter. For this workbook, however, we have added a fourth "R." It represents *reinforcement,* i.e., reinforcing your new, revised, positive messages with music and your choice of two other methods of communication we have studied. (We will walk you through this!)

It is the desire of the author that this chapter be simple, precise, to the point, and deeply impactful! This is not an unrealistic expectation, because it often happens that way when we get to this stage in our Reparenting Seminar.

The simplicity is in the fact that every child experiences impressionable times that leave indelible memory traces. For some reason, whatever is communicated to the child during such moments stays with the child and follows him or her into adulthood. We all have this in common.

The preciseness may be seen in the clear-cut, inner messages that result from these impressions. They may be good or bad, positive or negative, but they somehow become precise value judgments about one's self-worth, competence, belongingness, or potential for success. They are usually framed as short, pointed statements like a child would construct, and they become an integral part of our self-talk. The concern here is with the negative ones, such as, "I am stupid," "I can't do anything right," and "I'm only as good as you think I am."

The point is that we believe these negative messages. They are imprinted on the tables of our hearts, and we repeat them to ourselves so convincingly that we begin to behave as though they were accurate and true. They eventually shape the "reality" to which we respond. And time alone will not change this.

The good news is that those messages can be replaced with positive, healthy, inner messages. This requires steps and a process, and the results are often impactful emotionally and behaviorally. That's what this chapter is about.

Input from Dr. G.

The negative messages that your inner child believes, repeats, and accepts as his or her "reality" came from significant others at impressionable times in your life as a child. Some might have been the result of a single incident when a few words were unfitly spoken at a time of vulnerability. Or the negative message may have been repeated and reinforced many times, on many occasions, and in many ways. For example, a negative attitude may have been transmitted nonverbally by facial expressions, body language, or voice tone. There are many creative ways in which negative messages may have been inserted into your child's belief system. And once inserted, they are difficult to *recognize, remove,* and *replace.*

A few real-life success stories, however, are often an effective way to loosen or dislodge some of them a little. Think of it like a child wiggling a loose tooth. She knows that it will eventually come out and a new one will replace it. That should be the effect of the following true stories.

The first testimony is by Mary Ann Bird. It was condensed from an article in *Guidepost Magazine.* It describes a single moment when one significant person spoke seven words that overcame years of negative messages and changed a little girl's life forever.

The Whisper Test

By Mary Ann Bird

I grew up knowing I was different, and I hated it. I was born with a cleft pallet and when I started school my classmates made it clear to me how I must look to others; a little girl with a misshapen lip, crooked nose, lopsided teeth and garbled speech.

When schoolmates would ask, "what happened to your lip?" I'd tell them I'd fallen and cut it on a piece of glass. Somehow it seemed more acceptable to have suffered an accident than to have been **born** different. I was convinced that no one outside my family could love me. Or even like me. Then I entered Mrs. Leonard's 2nd grade class.

Mrs. Leonard was round and pretty and fragrant, with shining brown hair and warm, dark, smiling eyes. Everyone adored her. But no one came to love her more than I did. And for a special reason.

The time came for the annual hearing tests given at our school. I could barely hear out of one ear and was not about to reveal something else that would single me out as different. So I cheated. The "whisper test" required each child to go to the classroom door, turn sideways, close one ear with a finger, while the teacher whispered something from her desk, which the child repeated. Then the same for the other ear. Nobody checked how tightly the untested ear was covered, so I merely pretended to block mine.

As usual, I was last. But all through the testing I wondered what Mrs. Leonard might say to me. I knew from previous years that the teacher whispered things like, "The sky is blue," or "Do you have new shoes?"

My time came. I turned my bad ear toward her, plugging up the other just enough to be able to hear. I waited, and then came the words that God had surely put into her mouth, seven words that changed my life forever.

Mrs. Leonard, the teacher I adored, said softly, **"I wish you were my little girl."**

Overcoming a Self-Destructive Message

An Actual Counseling Case

The second testimony is an actual situation that required professional counseling to recognize, remove, and replace a negative message.

The owner of a large construction company brought his son for counseling. The owner was in his sixties, and the son was in his mid-thirties. The presentation problem was as follows.

The owner was wanting to retire. He had been grooming his son to take over and run the business. The son was intelligent, seemed to have good social skills, and reportedly had adequate knowledge and ability to run the business. The problem was that every few months he would do something "stupid" (to use their word) that would cost the company thousands of dollars or cause them to lose a major contract. This was puzzling to both the father and the son, because the son managed everything adequately and efficiently most of the time.

During the process of counseling, we discovered the problem. It stemmed from an incident between the father and the son when the son was eight or nine years old. It seems that the young boy had become negligent about his chores around the house and had become somewhat irresponsible regarding his school work. His mother asked his dad (who was not at home a lot because of his work) to have a talk with their son. He did, and during that conversation, he meant to tell his son that if he did not become more dependable and responsible, when he grew up, he would not be able to be a good father and would not be able to run the family business successfully.

Unfortunately, it had come across to the son as though the father were saying, "You will never be able to be as successful as I am." At least, this was the residual effect of their conversation. More than twenty-five years later, at a level below his conscious awareness, the son still believed that no matter how hard he tried, he could never be as successful as his father.

Since the son believed this negative message, it became a self-fulfilling prophecy. Therefore, every time he would approach the level of success that would allow him to replace his father as head of the company, he would somehow sabotage himself with an unwise business decision. Thus, he continued to demonstrate the behavior that verified the negative message he believed.

Through professional counseling, he and his father *recognized* the inner, negative message by recalling the conversation from which it stemmed. Through accessing the son's belief system, the false belief that perpetuated the negative message was identified and *removed*. Finally, through prayer, Scripture, and some inner child work, the old, negative message was *replaced* with new, positive, healthy messages based on the truth about the son's abilities, knowledge, experience, and personal potential.

As a result, the son was freed from the bondage of repeated failure and was eventually able to operate, take over, and expand the family business successfully. A few months later, the father was able to retire.

Taking It Personally

Use the information presented in this chapter thus far to fill in the blanks below. This exercise will prepare you to make personal applications in the section that follows:

1. What are The Three Rs Ramona likes to refer to in describing the process of dealing with negative, internal messages? Answer: R _____, R _____, and R _____ the negative messages with positive ones.

2. For this workbook, we have added a fourth "R." It represents _____ your new, revised, positive messages with _____ and with your choice of _____ other methods of communication we have already studied.

3. Every child experiences _____ moments that leave indelible _____ traces that stay with the child and follow him or her into adulthood.

4. These impressions may become precise value judgments about one's _____, competence, belongingness, or potential for _____.

5. These value judgments are usually framed as short, pointed statements like a _____ would construct, and they become an integral part of our _____.

6. The concern here is with the negative ones, such as the following example: _____ _____ .

7. The point is that we believe these messages, and we repeat them to ourselves so convincingly that we begin to _____ as though they were accurate and _____.

8. These messages eventually begin to shape the "_____" to which we respond. And time alone does _____ change this.

9. Some of these messages may have come from a _____ spoken incident. Or a negative attitude may have been repeated many times nonverbally by _____ expressions, _____ language, or _____ tones.

10. The first story described a single moment when one _____ person spoke one positive sentence that overcame years of negative messages. The second story was an actual situation that required _____ _____ in order to recognize, remove, and replace a negative message.

Recognizing Your Negative Messages

You should now be ready for the first "R," namely, *recognize* a few of your own negative, inner messages.

Following are some of the negative messages that are most frequently recognized. Place a checkmark by any of them that you probably should admit to and claim as your own. Feel free to change or revise the wording slightly to make the statement more accurate for you personally. Space has been left between the items for this purpose if you need it.

_____1. I am stupid.

_____2. I can't do anything right.

_____3. I'm only as good as you think I am.

_____4. Whatever I do is just not good enough.

_____5. I am a failure.

_____6. I am hopeless.

_____7. I am just a loser.

_____8. Nobody could really love me.

_____9. I'll never amount to anything.

_____10. I am never enough.

_____11. I don't deserve to be happy.

_____12. I can never be as successful as _____.

_____13. If people really knew me, they wouldn't like me.

_____14. My ideas are not worth much.

_____15. I should not expect much from myself.

_____16. Nobody really wants me around.

_____17. I just don't belong.

_____18. I am a mistake.

_____19. I am only worth what I have recently accomplished.

_____20. I will never fit in.

_____21. I should never have been born.

_____22. I am incompetent.

_____23. No one will ever really understand me.

_____24. Even God has it in for me.

_____25. Not even God could really love me.

Continue to think and pray that God will reveal any additional negative messages that you need to recognize and claim. Use the space below to list any others that He reveals:

_____

_____

_____

_____

Look over all the messages you have checked or listed. In the space below, write three or four of them that seem to be the deepest or the most hurtful to you. In other words, list three or four that you feel are in greatest need of being revised, removed, or replaced.

_____

_____

_____

_____

Removing Your Negative Messages

You should now be ready for the second "R," namely, *remove* some negative, inner messages. This process of removal usually involves critiquing, tweaking, and deleting. Examine the wording of the three or four statements you selected. Ask yourself if the present wording of the statements adequately expresses your inner, negative messages. This is your opportunity to revise or re-word a statement to make it more accurate or expressive for you personally.

There are actually three categories of negative messages that may need your consideration (or re-consideration). The first category has to do with actual personal handicaps or limitations that may cause a negative, inner message to contain an element of truth. For example, a physical condition may justify the statement, "I will never be able to run and play like other children do." This fact, however, does not justify other negative assumptions, such as, "I will never be successful, popular, happy, wealthy, or productive." Neither must the person necessarily conclude that he or she is (and always will be) a failure, a misfit, a loser, an outcast, unlovable, or hopeless.

There are thousands of biographies, autobiographies, and testimonies to prove that the fact of a personal handicap or limitation is not the real problem with which we are dealing. The real problem results from an attitude toward one's self that discourages achievement, undermines self-worth, assassinates hope, and immobilizes progress towards one's true potential. It is important, therefore, that you differentiate between the fact of an actual handicap or limitation and the debilitating effect of a negative attitude based on a false belief.

Take a few moments now to examine the three or four messages you listed earlier to see if any of them are statements of actual handicaps or limitations. If so, please understand that such a statement of accurate fact does not qualify as a negative message based on a false belief. It is the debilitating, devaluating assumptions *about* the condition that must be dealt with here. Be sure you get this point, because you may need to re-word or totally disregard one (or more) of the messages you listed if it is in this category.

Use the space below to discuss any such changes you may need to make because of this category. Feel free to explain why you may choose to reword, disregard, or delete one (or more) of the messages you listed.

_____

_____

_____

_____

There is a second category of negative messages you may be able to omit or delete. These are the ones that do not pass the "sanity check" because they are based on an unreasonable assumption or unrealistic expectation.

For example, consider the following negative message:

"I can never be as successful as _____."

If you put Donald Trump's name in the blank, your message would likely fail the "sanity check." It is not reasonable for about 99 percent of our population to expect to be as financially successful as Donald Trump. Do you really think that you should feel bad about yourself if you do not achieve his economic status? Probably not.

Try filling the blank above with the following names, and then do a "sanity check" to determine if the statement is based on a realistic or unrealistic expectation:

Bill Gates	Billy Graham
Elvis Presley	Tiger Woods
Mother Theresa	Rudolph (the reindeer)

Once again, review your three or four negative statements to see if any of them are based on assumptions or expectations that are unreasonable or unrealistic for you. If so, they do not pass the "sanity check" and must be omitted.

Sometimes there is an "aha" moment when you can suddenly see the faulty assumption on which a negative message is based. If you experienced such a moment of insight, describe it below.

_____

_____

_____

_____

The third category of messages consists of the ones that are in direct conflict with a clear statement of Scripture. For many Bible-believing Christians, a clear statement of Scripture that cleanly disputes and refutes a negative, inner message is enough to justify deleting the negative message promptly and precisely. In such cases, all that may be needed is the experience of facing and processing the irresolvable conflict between your negative message and the biblical truth. This can simply and sometimes quickly produce a "showdown" that requires a logical decision! Are you going to accept the scriptural truth or your false belief? To which are you going to commit? You *will* make a choice!

A few examples follow:

False, Negative Message	Scriptural Truth
God has forsaken me.	God has promised that He will never leave you nor forsake you (Hebrews 13:5).
My life has no purpose.	God says that He has plans for you—plans for good and not for evil (Jeremiah 29:11).
I should never have been born.	He chose you before the foundation of the world (Ephesians 1:4).

Examine your remaining negative statements to see if any of them are in direct conflict with a clear statement of Scripture. You may need to consult with a minister, a Christian counselor, or a friend who knows the Bible well in order to complete this exercise effectively.

If you find any negative statements that directly conflict with clear scriptural truth, write them below, and tell how they conflict with Scripture. *If you are among the few who do not find any remaining conflicting, negative statements, you may skip all the way to the section entitled "Application."* Most of us will need to continue with this exercise.

_____

_____

_____

_____

Think about how it will affect you if you reject the false, negative message(s) and accept scriptural struth. What difference will it make? What thoughts, attitudes, beliefs, or behaviors would you have to change? Discuss this below.

_____

_____

_____

_____

You are now facing a "showdown," and you must make a decision. It would obviously be best to use your will to consciously reject the conflicting message and accept scriptural truth. Use the following procedure and acknowledgment to help you do this.

1. Read the acknowledgment below silently, and think about what it means.
2. Ask God to help you apply it in your mind, emotions, and belief system.
3. Make the actual conscious decision to follow through on this.
4. Follow through by reading the acknowledgment aloud and then signing it. (It would probably be most effective to read it aloud in the presence of someone you trust, and then have that person also sign below to validate and emotionally mark the occasion.)

"I acknowledge that the negative message written above directly conflicts with scriptural truth and that the Bible clearly disputes and refutes it. On that basis, I hereby choose to reject it, to resist its influence on my thinking, to adjust my attitude and behavior accordingly, and to receive God's grace to make this decision a reality in my life."

Signature _____ Date _____

Signature of someone you trust (optional): "I hereby witness, validate, and emotionally mark the decision acknowledged above."

Signature _____ Date _____

Replacing Your Negative Messages

You have *recognized* and *removed* some of your negative, inner messages. Simply removing some of them, however, may create a vacuum into which other negative messages may collect or accumulate. Like a dentist filling a tooth, the decay must be removed, but the job is not complete until the cavity is filled with some good, safe, healthy, permanent material. Then there must still be some polishing and maintenance. Likewise, you should be prepared for the third "R," namely *replacing* the negative messages with positive ones.

Begin by listing below any of your negative messages that have survived the section on removing. In other words, use the space below to express a few (no more than three) of your negative messages that still remain after critiquing, tweaking, and deleting. If you revised or reworded any of them, express them in their final form.

_____

_____

_____

_____

Now, examine your first remaining negative statement. Ask yourself what truth(s) or positive statement(s) you would need to accept in order to refute, correct, or counteract that negative message. Carefully word the positive statement(s) that would effectively replace the negative one, and write it (them) below.

_____

_____

_____

_____

Next, do the same for the second remaining negative statement that you listed above (if any), and write below the resulting positive statement(s) that will effectively replace it.

_____

_____

_____

_____

Finally, do the same for the third remaining negative statement that you listed above (if any), and write below the resulting positive statement(s) that will effectively replace it.

_____

_____

_____

_____

Now give some thought to the person or people you would have liked most to have said those words to you when you were a child. In other words, consider the positive statements one at a time, and ask yourself this question: "From whom would my little, inner child have liked to hear these words truthfully spoken?" Write your answers below. (If you cannot come up with answers that seem probable or plausible to you, then ask your inner child by using one of the methods of communication you learned in Chapters 11 and 13, and describe this experience also in the space below.)

_____

_____

_____

_____

In some cases, the actual person (people) you mentioned may still be alive, accessible, and able to say those very things to you in the present. Discuss below whether or not this might be a feasible or reasonable thing to pursue. Why or why not?

_____

_____

_____

_____

If you decide to pursue the idea of hearing those positive words in the present from the actual person (people) you would have wanted/needed to hear them from in the past, use the space below to describe your plans, your process, and your results. Some people have been able to do this effectively and successfully.

_____

_____

_____

_____

Finally, accept the fact that ultimately, you, the adult, must accept the responsibility for correcting the false, negative messages that your little, inner child believes and includes in his or her self-talk. You must design a strategy to accomplish this, and you probably will need to use several of the methods of communication that you learned in Chapters 11 and 13.

Use the following checklist to achieve this crucial goal. Put your initials after each item after it has been completed.

1. Read the following story entitled "Now It's Your Turn!" _____ *(Initial.)*
2. Read and study the section of this chapter entitled, "Little Mona Did It." Focus on how she did this exercise. _____ *(Initial.)*
3. Review chapter 13, including your answer to the question regarding methods of communication that work best for you and your inner child. _____ *(Initial.)*
4. Begin to design your strategy by completing the ten sentences which follow the story. _____ *(Initial.)*

"Now It's Your Turn"

I'm not sure where I heard this story or who wrote it. I may have read it in one of the old *Chicken Soup* books. The best I can remember, it was about a little girl who was very close to her grandfather. They laughed and played a lot together. Throughout her childhood, he called her "the Princess," and he was constantly affirming her and building her self-esteem through things that he would say and do.

When she was a young adult, her grandfather passed away. She missed him greatly and grieved his death intensely. A few weeks later, she had a dream. In the dream, she saw her grandfather standing by her bed. He had a familiar smile on his face. He looked at her and said, "Now it is your turn. You will have to do it now." And then she woke up.

She was puzzled by the dream and wondered what it meant. What is it now her turn to do? She looked up at a picture of her and her grandfather on the wall. It was taken when she was a child. In the picture, he was holding a banner that said, "Happy birthday, Princess." He had that same familiar smile on his face. Suddenly she understood.

The message of the dream was to her as an adult. It was now her turn to affirm the little girl inside herself. She, the adult, would now have to be the one to remind her little, inner child that she is still important, still valuable, and still "the Princess." She must now assume this responsibility.

Design your strategy by completing the following sentences.

1. In the final paragraph of the story entitled "Now It's Your Turn," the lady finally understood her responsibility to/for:

    _____

    _____

    _____

    _____

2. Like the lady in the story, my personal strategy must begin with the realization that I too am responsible to/for:

    _____

    _____

    _____

    _____

3. When I read and studied the section of this chapter entitled "Little Mona Did It," I was impressed by:

_____

_____

_____

_____

4. Something I remember from "Little Mona Did It" that might help me design my own strategy or experience is:

_____

_____

_____

_____

5. After I reviewed my Chapter 13 responses, I decided to use the following methods of communication with my inner child in the strategy I am designing:

_____

_____

_____

_____

6. From Chapter 14, I have concluded that the most important (two or three) positive statements to get into the self-talk of my inner child are:

_____

_____

_____

_____

7. One idea for using a specific method of communication to emphasize or input a specific positive statement into the self-talk of my inner child is:

_____

_____

_____

_____

8. A second idea for using a specific method of communication to emphasize or input a specific positive statement into the self-talk of my inner child is:

_____

_____

_____

_____

9. A third idea for using a specific method of communication to emphasize or input a specific positive statement into the self-talk of my inner child is:

_____

_____

_____

_____

10. I will commit to actually use the three ideas above (or some variations thereof) at the times and places selected below:

    a. First idea: Date _____ Place _____

    b. Second idea: Date _____ Place _____

    c. Third idea: Date _____ Place _____

Initial here when all three ideas have been used/experienced:

How did your three ideas work out? What were the experiences like? What were some of your thoughts or feelings as you were doing the activities? Was there anything difficult, surprising, or impressive about the entire experience? Use the space below to discuss or respond to these questions:

_____

_____

_____

_____

Reinforcing Your Positive Messages

Often in video games, there are opportunities to save your progress. If you do not take advantage of those opportunities, you will have to start over from the beginning (or at most, from your previous save point) the next time you play the game. Likewise, you must reinforce your new, revised, positive messages, or your progress will be at risk. In other words, you may lose the ground you have worked so hard to gain.

Reinforcement Step Number One is writing a paragraph of positive self-talk. Do this by expressing your three new, positive messages in a conversational way, using words that would be understandable to a child (your inner child). Include some scriptural or logical reasons why those positive messages should be accepted as truth. Don't make this exercise difficult. Simple is better!

For example, if my original negative self-talk included the false belief that said, "Not even God could really love me," the revised, positive message is that God *does* really love me. A scriptural reason for accepting the positive message as truth is John 3:16: "For God so loved the world that He gave His only begotten Son...." Two logical reasons for accepting this truth are: (1) I choose to believe the Bible. (2) If God "so loved" the world, the word *world* includes me! In other words, I can substitute my own name into that verse and choose to accept it as truth.

Another common example is the original, negative self-talk that begins with the following false belief: "Everyone would like me, if only I...." There are hundreds of ways to finish this sentence, and all of them are wrong! No matter how you finish this sentence, it will still be a false belief. The thing that makes it false is the word *everyone*. The revised, positive message is this: no matter how you are, some people will like you, and some others will not like you. A scriptural reason for accepting this positive message as truth is Matthew 5:11, which says that even if you were perfect, some people would not like you (would persecute you) because of your righteousness. Logical reasons to accept the positive statement can be seen all around you. A reality check will reveal this truth at school, at work, and even at church.

I will give you a third example because you will probably be using three positive statements of your own in this assignment. In this example, the original, negative self-talk is: "I can't do anything right," or "I can't do anything as well as other people." The revised, positive message is as follows: "There is something— maybe several things— that I can do as well as most people and better than some!" Some scriptural reasons for accepting this positive message center around the fact that God has gifted each of His children uniquely, with the very abilities that He wants us to use in His wonderful plan for our lives. Some of the verses that declare this truth are Jer. 29:11; 1 Cor. 12:11,18,22; 1 Peter 4:10-11; Eph. 4:7,11,16. A logical reason could be the fact that a tall person can do better at the high jump, but the short guy can win at limbo almost every time! You get the idea. "The eye cannot say unto the hand, I have no need of thee ..." (1 Cor. 12:21).

So, let us use these three positive messages to provide an example of Reinforcement Step Number One, i.e., a paragraph of conversational self-talk. Such a paragraph might go something like this: "I need to accept the truth that God really does love me. Since I accept the Bible as the Word of God, I will also accept the truth that 'God so loved the world...' and that includes me! I have also learned that no matter what kind of person I choose to be, there will be some people who will like me and some who will not. So, I will choose to be a good person and will appreciate the people who like me and not worry about the ones who don't. Also, I now realize that there is something—maybe several things—that I can do as well as most people and better than some. I accept the fact that God has given all of His children certain abilities that He wants us to use in His wonderful plan for our lives. I will remind myself of these truths regularly, until they become a part of my automatic self-talk."

Tom's Example:

Tom's three original, false, negative messages were the ones mentioned earlier in this chapter, which follow:

1. God has forsaken me.
2. My life has no purpose.
3. I should never have been born.

His new, positive statements designed to replace the old, negative messages are as follows:

1. In Hebrew 13:5, God promised that He would never leave me nor forsake me.
2. In Jeremiah 29:11, God says that He has plans for me—plans for good and not for evil.
3. In Ephesian 1:4, God says that He chose me long before I was ever born.

The paragraph he wrote to put these positive, new messages into conversational form was as follows: "I now understand that God will never forsake or abandon me. He promised this in His Word. He also said that He has a purpose for my life, that His plans for me are good, and that He planned all this for me long before I was born. This means that I was no accident and that it will be an exciting adventure to watch God unfold His plans and purpose for my life! I choose to believe this and to remind myself of it often."

Use the space below to compose your own paragraph of conversational self-talk, using scriptural or logical reasons why your three new, positive statements should be accepted as truth.

_____

_____

_____

_____

Application

Reinforcement Step Number Two is: internalize the paragraph of conversational, positive self-talk that you composed (above). You should do this through the following process:

1. Read it aloud at least twice a day for at least ten days. It is important that you hear your own voice using those exact words repeatedly during that period of time. This applies three biblical principles. One is that faith comes by hearing (Rom. 10:17). The second is that what you confess with your mouth becomes a "done deal" in your heart (Rom. 10:10). The third is that repetition reinforces, i.e., "line upon line, precept upon precept" (Is. 28:10). This helps it to become "written on the tables of your heart" (2 Cor. 3:3).

2. Write your paragraph by hand. Take your time, and use your best handwriting. Tape this onto the top, right corner of your vanity mirror, slightly above your line of vision. Then, a few days later, write the same paragraph with your opposite (non-dominant) hand. Tape this onto the top, left corner of your vanity mirror, slightly above your line of vision. Leave both of these posted on your vanity mirror for at least a month. (You'll get a little extra subliminal benefit from this.)

3. Try to locate some songs that reinforce the truths of your paragraph. This is not as hard as it may sound. You simply have to pay attention to the words of some songs. A good place to start might be a hymnal, especially one that contains some hymns you became familiar with as a child. For example, if I were trying to overcome the negative message that *God has forsaken me* and replace it with the positive message that *God promised not to leave me nor forsake me*, I would look up an old hymn I learned in my childhood entitled "Never Alone." The chorus goes like this:

> No, never alone. No, never alone.
> He promised never to leave me,
> Never to leave me alone.
> No, never alone. No, never alone.
> He promised never to leave me,
> Never to leave me alone.

There are also some secular songs that can help. Long ago, when I was trying to replace the false belief that I should expect everyone to love and accept me, a song became popular that helped me. The guy on the recording was singing, "If you don't like me, kindly pass me by...." He didn't seem at all upset or even surprised that some people did not like him. I thought, "What a great way to look at it!" So, I chuckled and sang along with him on the chorus, "Pass me by, pass me by, if you don't happen to like me, pass me by!" Soon, I had replaced the old, negative message with a healthier insight: *No matter how I am or choose to be, some people will like me, and some people will not. That's the way it is, and it's OK!*

An old country-western song that was helpful to a young man after his girlfriend "dumped" him starts like this: "I got along without-cha … before I met-cha … I'm gonna get along without-cha now!"

A more contemporary song that could encourage a believer in times of trouble and reinforce the positive message to look ahead is entitled "What Could Be Better?" It was recorded by a group called 33 Miles. Some of the lyrics follow:

> I'm livin' in the days ahead.
> I'm already dancin' on the streets of gold,
> And I can't stop celebrating in my soul.
> 'Cause I'm livin' in the days ahead.
> Nothing on earth could ever compare.
> I can't wait for the day that I get there.
> When I see Jesus face to face,
> Tell me what could be better.
> Tell me what could be better.

Here is one more example. A children's song by Bill and Gloria Gaither has validated a lot of people whose self-image needed a boost. The title is "I'm Somebody," and the chorus gives four reasons why.

> I'm somebody; yes, I'm somebody.
> I'm created in the image of God
>   and I'm somebody.
> I'm somebody; I said somebody.
>   I am loved.
>   I am His child.
>   I'm important to Him!

Use the space below to list the titles of at least three songs that might help to reinforce the truths of the paragraph you wrote.

_____

_____

_____

_____

Write out or summarize any particular words, ideas, or lyrics that caused you to select these songs.

_____

_____

_____

_____

4. Listen to and/or sing the songs you selected until you know them very well. In fact, play them for background music at times when you really aren't paying much attention to them. You may need to make your own recordings of these songs so that you can play them repeatedly, one after the other, as you drive or even while you are sleeping. Continue this for at least two weeks, even if you get tired of hearing them. When you are so saturated that you are no longer paying conscious attention to the lyrics, there is still a residual effect that will help reinforce the positive message.

When you have finished this assignment, initial and date below.

When you have finished this assignment, initial and date below.

_____   _____
         Initial   Date

Transitional Point: *Scripturally there are eight purposes for which God gave us music. The way we are using it in the process of reparenting is in keeping with these purposes. If you are interested in more information about the "Eight Biblical Purposes for Music," contact Dr. Larry Gilliam at Dayspring Counseling Services in Irving, Texas.*

Little Mona Did It

Replacing those negative messages from childhood and adolescence has been a long, hard task, and it has required a major conscious effort on my part. I do not mean to sound pessimistic, but this world is not a healthy place, and finding healthy, supportive people is not easy!

While I was struggling to recover and heal, it seemed that people were standing in line to tell me all my character defects (as if I wasn't all too aware of them). I often wanted to give up, thinking, "They are right, it's not worth it; I'm not worth it!" It took a lot of encouragement from Dr. G., but we finally found a little part of me that would agree that "I AM worth it!" I don't know if it was stubbornness or determination, but that part of me kept on working and fighting until she could honestly proclaim, "I AM worth it, and I WILL make it!"

The negative message that I struggled with most of all was, "I'm just not good enough!" My feelings of inadequacy were sometimes overwhelming. I found that it would help a little if I made a list of my accomplishments. I started naming and listing specific incidents when I helped other people, made someone laugh, or wrote a poem that touched someone's heart. I consciously began trying to develop these good points about myself.

One day I shared some of my poetry with my friend Sue. When I finished, she looked at me and said, "I wish I could write like you do." Suddenly, I felt really good inside. I don't think it was a pride thing. I think I realized that my writing had connected with another human being. She could relate to it, understand it, and appreciate it. It wasn't in flowery words or phrases, but it touched her life; and in a way, her response touched and changed my life.

Then there was the time in an inpatient psychiatric setting when I think I really helped someone. The girl who was my roommate had a paranoid episode, became terrified, ran somewhere, and hid. Everyone was looking for her. Finally, we found her huddled in a corner on the floor, too terrified to move. The staff allowed me to walk over and sit with her on the floor. For about an hour, I reassured her that she was safe, that the "things" she feared were sent away, and that I would not allow anything or anyone to hurt her. Finally, she looked up at me and said, "I trust you!"

At that moment, I felt that she had given me a gift so precious that I almost cried! I said, "Let's go eat a snack!' We got up and went into the dining room together.

The real point is, I knew that I had done something good, and I gave myself credit for it. It was almost like I had finally received my certification as a human being.

Gradually, I stopped berating myself so much. Shaming my inner child didn't work when my mother did it, and it didn't work when I did it to myself either. Shame never made me want to change. It just convinced me that I was hopelessly bad and *could not* change. These days I understand that my sins or my mistakes are not who *I am*, but what *I do*! I accept myself as a whole person, unique but capable of both good and bad. I am OK with that, because that's the way we human beings are on this earth.

I no longer have to be the best or the worst or the sickest. I get to be a person, and I get to be *me*! I am glad that I traded in a lot of negative messages for positive ones! I now accept the whole package of who I was, who I am, and who God says I will be someday, for His honor and glory!

Would you like to join me? There is room!

Chapter 15

Learning How to "Manage" Your Inner Child

Vantage Point

ONCE AGAIN, LET us consult the Process Checklist to clarify our next step and to be sure we are facing the right direction!

That checklist expresses the goals of Chapter Fifteen as follows:

- Item 24: Explore what it would mean for you (the adult) to "manage" or parent your inner child.
- Item 25: Design an on-going strategy for "managing" or parenting your inner child.

Notice that you are supposed to *explore* something and *design* something. Examine Item 24 above, and write below what you are supposed to explore:

_____

_____

_____

_____

Examine Item 25 above, and write below what you are supposed to design:

_____

_____

_____

_____

Let's let The Kid participate in the next exercise. We might as well have a little fun while we clarify our perspective!

Put your pen in your non-dominant hand, and let The Kid print "EXPLORE" from top to bottom in the space below, to form an acrostic at the left margin. (Let the adult help, if necessary).

_____

_____

_____

_____

Next, let the adult read the following seven points we will cover as we "explore" something:

1. Pay attention to the uniqueness of your inner child.
2. Raise your level of relationship on the G-scale Hierarchy of Importance.
3. Observe and apply the principles of the Baseball Diamond Model.
4. Learn the management style that will work best for you.
5. X-clude (or "X out") some myths about parenting.
6. Explain why good reparenting requires "managing" the child.
7. Examine the factors you have explored so far in this chapter.

These seven points give you an overview, but they are not listed here in the right order. To see the sequence in which they will be covered in this chapter, you must match the first letter of each sentence with the letters of the EXPLORE acrostic that you printed with your non-dominant hand.

With your pen in your usual writing hand, copy each of the seven points next to the appropriate letter of the EXPLORE acrostic. (Note: The sentence starting with the word *Examine* goes last.)

Regarding your assignment to design an ongoing strategy, please humor the author by reading the following sentence aloud: "My job is to decide on the kind of experience and the style of relationship I will use to manage, guide, and continue to nurture my inner child."

Thank you. Now, involve The Kid once again by figuring out how to divide the sentence you just read so that it fits the DESIGN acrostic format shown below. Omit the first four words ("My job is to ..."), and the rest of each sentence will fit perfectly into the DESIGN acrostic exactly as it is worded!

Decide ____ ____ ____ ____

Experience ____ ____

Style ____ _____

I ____ ____ ____ _____,

Guide, ____ _____ ____

Nurture ____ _____ ____.

Thanks again. You're a good sport!

By now, you have probably gained your perspective and clarified your Vantage Point for Chapter Fifteen. An additional by-product of this unusual introduction to a new chapter may be the emergence of your inner adolescent. That is the term we will apply to the part of you that may be feeling irritated (if not insulted) by the exercises you just completed. Your inner adolescent may consider this portion of the chapter as childish busy work and a waste of time. The adult may tend to agree but may also suspect that the author probably has a subtle reason for starting the chapter differently from the others. (The adult would be right!)

Input from Dr. G.

Explain why good parenting requires "managing" the child.

The first car I ever owned definitely needed "managing!" It was an old, used car that had apparently been in a wreck before I got it, and one of its characteristics was this: It pulled to the right. If I gave the steering wheel any slack, the car actually took off to the right. Where I grew up, that usually meant it was headed for the ditch! I constantly had to compensate for this tendency by holding the steering wheel a little to the left. As I think back on this, I feel sure that I traveled down the road at some kind of angle, which probably amused the old-timers in my hometown (especially the spit-and-whittle bunch who often sat on a bench in front of my dad's grocery store). But at least I was "managing my old jalopy!" (Does anyone use that word anymore?)

Since we've all been "dented" in some way along the road of life, we're probably all a little out of alignment in one way or another. A part of our uniqueness and individuality is due to the nature and intensity of our "fender-benders" and the ways we have tried to compensate for our respective misalignments.

Of course, not every pre-owned vehicle needs the same kind of management as my first car. Likewise, not every inner child needs (or will respond to) the same style of reparenting.

The fact remains, however, that every inner child requires some management by the adult. Otherwise, you have a situation much like leaving a small child without supervision. Or even worse, the situation might be likened to a small child being allowed to run a household or a business.

Realize also that you cannot get rid of your inner child. He or she will remain with you throughout your life, along with whatever attitudes, issues, and emotional baggage happen to be attached. You can't spank The Kid and hand it off to a babysitter or put it up for adoption. You can't even tie it up, gag it, or lock it in its room. You are stuck with that part of yourself, and your only viable option is to learn to manage it. In other words, without management, the tail will surely wag the dog!

Think about all this for a moment, and then explain in your own words why good reparenting requires managing your inner child:

_____

_____

_____

_____

X-clude (or "X out") some myths about parenting.

There are many ideas about parenting that seem right and sound right, but they are not right. To believe or practice these myths would be a "myth-stake."

Read the statements that follow. Put an *X* in the blank after each statement you believe is a myth, i.e., not true or not good parenting. Put a checkmark after each statement you believe is true or represents good parenting for you.

1. Parents automatically know what is best for their own children. _____

2. If a person is old enough to have a child, he or she must be mature enough to be a good parent. _____

3. Most parents will think back through their own childhood and objectively decide which parenting practices they will use with their own children. _____

4. An adult who was abused as a child is not likely to abuse his/her own children. _____

5. Children should be expected to love and respect their parents, no matter what. _____

6. A good parenting strategy is to think of children as miniature adults. _____

7. A parenting approach that works with one child will usually work with other children, especially if they are in the same family. _____

8. A parent should show the child who is boss by shouting louder than the child. _____

9. Children usually understand their underlying needs and can tell their parents what they really need if the parents will only listen. _____

10. It is more important to focus on a child's faults than to point out and foster his/her good points. _____

11. It is important to convince our children that their ideas and opinions are immature and should not be expressed. _____

12. A good way to control a child is to use shame, i.e., saying, "Shame on you!" or, "You should be ashamed of yourself!" _____

13. An effective parenting tool is to take advantage of the child's fears. The child will respect the parent who keeps him sufficiently afraid. _____

14. Good parenting requires clearly stated rules that are strictly enforced with well-defined consequences and with no exceptions. _____

15. Good parenting will result in a child who will meet the parent's needs and expectations. _____

16. If you force a child to say the right words, his or her feelings will eventually line up with what he or she says. _____

17. A good way to discipline a child is to withdraw attention or withhold affection until he/she straightens up. _____

18. The amount of anger a parent feels is a good indicator of how severely a child's punishment should be. _____

19. It is more important for a parent to relate to his/her child as a friend than as a parent. _____

20. It is important for the parent to always have the last word when a child is argumentative.

———

Will you be surprised to find out that all twenty of the statements above are myths? It is a fact that *none* of the twenty statements above represent good parenting. Exclude them all as you plan your management strategy for your inner child.

If some of those statements sounded good to you, and you disagree with our assessment of them, please consider the following comments about each of the twenty statements:

1. The truth is that parents do not automatically have a built-in manual regarding what is best for their children. Study of biblical principles, parenting research, and advice from successful and experienced parents are necessary and wise. Natural instincts are not enough.

2. The fact that a person has reached puberty certainly does not guarantee mature thinking, good judgment, or knowledge about caring for children.

3. Most parents will tend to parent the way they were parented, even if they claim to disagree with it. The power of what was modeled for us at impressionable times is amazing in its impact. A small percentage of parents may objectively decide on their parenting practices.

4. Strangely enough, most abusive parents were themselves victims of childhood abuse. There is a book entitled *Hurt People Hurt People*.

5. The tricky part of this sentence is "should be expected." Even if children should always love and respect their parents, no matter what, the reality is that they often do not; so it would be unrealistic to always expect them to, no matter what.

6. To think of children as miniature adults totally disregards their developmental stages, the normal characteristics of each stage, and what is (or is not) age-appropriate.

7. Parenting approaches should be geared to the individual differences of each child. Often children in the same family are very different from each other in a number of ways, including styles of learning.

8. There are better ways to assert your authority than shouting down your child.

9. Children cannot be expected to understand their underlying needs. Even if they understood them, they would probably not be able to verbalize them.

10. Positive reinforcement—emphasizing and fostering their good points—is healthier and more effective.

11. While children should be taught to respect authority, it is desirable for children to know that they are important and have a significant place in the total family system. This means that there should be a time, an opportunity, and a defined manner in which they may safely express their ideas and opinions, even if they are immature.

12. To heap shame onto a child is a terrible error. It often becomes an issue that assassinates hope and follows the child into adulthood.

13. Childhood fears will normally and naturally drive a child toward his or her parents for protection and comfort. The best parenting is to relate to the child as a source of safety and security. This will calm the fears, keep them rational, and help avoid a multitude of fear-driven issues when the child reaches adulthood.

14. The untrue part of this statement is the phrase "with no exceptions." You don't want to completely rule out the possibility that some set of circumstances could arise that would justify some negotiation or creative alternative that is better than the original consequence. Sometimes it is better to err on the side of grace than on the side of legalism.

15. Obviously, the primary purpose of parenting is not to meet the needs and expectations of the parents. Even if it were, that would not be an appropriate way to define good parenting.

16. There is an element of truth in this, such as requiring a young child to say, "I'm sorry." But there is no guarantee that the child will automatically begin to mean it.

17. To withhold affection or attention from a child for any extended period of time deprives the child of a basic, primal need and may raise more problems than it solves. For example, it can teach a performance-based acceptance, foster an unhealthy perfectionism, and result in a self-image deficit.

18. The amount of anger felt by a parent tells you more about the parent than about the appropriate punishment of the child. If anything, the parent should not discipline the child at all while feeling angry.

19. It would be nice to be friend and parent, but sometimes these roles are mutually exclusive. At times when you can't be both, the role of parent trumps the role of friend!

20. When a sentence contains the word *always*, it is usually going to be untrue. While normal respect would give the parent the final word, there are times when the parent would be wise to simply walk away without honoring a child's comment with a response.

Are there any of the twenty statements that still seem to you to be good parenting? If so, explain which one(s) and why. (It is OK for you to disagree, if you can defend your position.)

_____

_____

_____

_____

Hopefully, this exercise has helped you recognize some myths to exclude from your reparenting strategy.

Pay attention to the uniqueness of your inner child.

A lady once noticed that her husband had gained a lot of weight. She said to him, "You need to get in shape!"

He replied, "Round is a shape!"

My point is that everyone is in some kind of shape, and that shape (whatever it is) must be taken into consideration as you determine an appropriate style of management for your inner child.

Pastor Rick Warren, in his best-selling book *The Purpose Driven Life,* used the following acrostic to explain the importance of knowing and understanding one's "SHAPE"[1]:

Spiritual gifts—Every believer has been endowed with at least one!
Heart—Whatever you are really passionate about.
Abilities—What you can perform, demonstrate, or do well.
Personality—See comments on temperament, which follow.
Experience—Ways in which life experiences have affected you.

Regarding spiritual gifts, here is some information that should be helpful to you in completing this exercise:

1. God does not want us to be ignorant regarding spiritual gifts (1 Cor. 12:1).
2. There are several different gifts He has distributed among us (1 Cor. 12:4–6).
3. Each is an expression of God's grace; it is not earned or deserved (Eph. 4:7).

---

[1]Rick Warren, *The Purpose Driven Life* (Grand Rapids, Michigan: Zondervan, 2002), 235–236.

4. He empowers each believer with at least one spiritual gift (1 Cor. 12:11).
5. He does not want us to neglect these gifts He has given us (1 Tim. 4:14).
6. He instructs us to "stir up" whatever gifts He has chosen to give us (2 Tim. 1:6).
7. He expects each believer to minister according to these giftings (1 Pet. 4:11).

Such abilities are spiritually energized and are not the same as natural talents. The seven spiritual gifts listed in Romans 12:6–8 are actually much like temperaments, in that they determine how people view life situations as well as how they may go about solving life's problems. For example, "the teacher" would probably approach a difficult situation differently than "the administrator." Likewise, the leader with "the prophet's temperament" will likely deal with people differently (more sternly) than "the mercy-shower." Accordingly, "the exhorter" will be more of an encourager, while "the liberal giver" will tend to see solutions in terms of financial resources or material things, i.e., the fiscal or the physical.

One benefit of knowing and understanding one's spiritual gifts may be seen in regard to the gift of discernment that is mentioned in 1 Corinthians 12:10. One of the effects of "discernment" is that the person with this gift is more sensitive to almost everything than the average person. People with the gift of discernment simply pick up more signals! They need to realize that others may not even notice certain things that may seem obvious and paramount to "the discerner."

These comments are not intended to be comprehensive or exhaustive regarding the subject of spiritual gifts. These few observations are included to emphasize the importance of understanding the unique individuality of your inner child as you determine his or her "SHAPE." If you would like more information regarding spiritual gifts, your best source is probably your Pastor. Or you may consult our Dayspring Counseling Services in Irving, Texas.

In Volume 1, Chapter 9 of this book, we introduced the importance of knowing and understanding the temperament of your inner child. We provided a simple way for you to identify your own primary and secondary temperaments and to get a feel for the legitimate strengths and weaknesses of each. In that chapter, we referred to temperament as a cluster of in-born, God-given tendencies that determine how we react to people, places, and things. Your *temperament* is more like your original "wiring," while *personality* seems to refer more to how that potential actually unfolded (or didn't) in response to the situations and circumstances of your life.

You may want to look back at Volume 1, Chapter 9 to remind yourself about your inner child's temperament. If so, use the space below to discuss any strengths and weaknesses you may want to remember when you design your strategy for managing your inner child.

_____

_____

_____

_____

To learn more about your temperament, you may arrange to take the Arno Profile System by contacting the National Christian Counselors Association at 5260 Paylor Lane, Sarasota, FL 34240, or visit their website at www.ncca.org.

Use the space below to discuss briefly how all the factors listed in the "SHAPE" acrostic may relate to your inner child. Try to include something you know about The Kid in each of the five categories that will help reveal the uniqueness of his or her "SHAPE." These comments will help in designing a style of management that is appropriate and effective.

S

_____

_____

H

_____

_____

A

_____

_____

P

_____

_____

E

_____

_____

Learn the management style that will work best for you.

I consulted several dictionaries and selected for our consideration the following definitions of "manage":

- To handle or treat with care
- To set limits or parameters for
- To guide, direct, or discipline
- To exercise administrative or supervisory control over
- To make submissive or keep in submission

I think I have listed these five definitions in order from the gentlest to the most harsh, or from the most permissive to the most demanding.

Do you agree? If not, then number the items above according to your opinion from the gentlest and most permissive (No. 1) to the most harsh and most demanding (No. 5). Explain below, if you wish.

_____

_____

_____

_____

In consideration of what you wrote about the unique "SHAPE" of your inner child, which one of the five management definitions above would seem to be appropriate and effective for your inner child most of the time? Why?

_____

_____

_____

_____

Which other one of the five management definitions might be necessary or appropriate for your inner child at times when your first approach does not seem to work? In other words, which style seems to be the second preference for managing your inner child? Why?

_____

_____

_____

_____

When might it be necessary to switch to this secondary style of managing your inner child? Explain below.

_____

_____

_____

_____

From the negative perspective, what would you like to remind yourself *not to do* in managing your inner child? In other words, what parenting style did *not work well* when your parent(s) tried it and probably will still not work well today in dealing with your inner child?

_____

_____

_____

_____

Observe and apply the principles of the Baseball Diamond Model.

On Career Day, a fifth-grade teacher was allowing her students to talk about the kinds of work their parents did. She was impressed when one little boy announced that his father was a diamond cutter! She began explaining the uniqueness of that profession, and the little boy interrupted. "Yes, Ma'am," he clarified, "my father mows the grass down at the baseball field!"

When we refer to the *Baseball Diamond Model,* we're talking about a baseball field and the way it is laid out. Almost everybody can picture in their minds the first base, second base, third base, and home base that make up the infield. If you can visualize this, you can learn the Baseball Diamond Model. The following diagram should help:

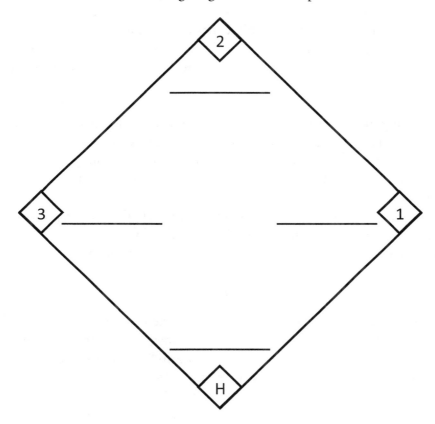

Example BD-1

It is important in baseball to run the bases in the proper order. There is a reason why they call a certain base *first* base. Hopefully, the runner will go there first! No matter how sincere you may be, or how far you hit the ball, if you touch the bases in the wrong order, you will be called out when you reach home! Likewise, in using the Baseball Diamond Model, the direction, order, and sequence of events are important.

In the blank next to *first base,* write the word *thoughts*. It is clear from Scripture and from research that this process begins with your thoughts. That's why Scripture says, "As he thinketh ... so is he" (Prov. 23:7). That's why we are told that change can occur when we "bring thoughts into captivity" (2 Cor. 10:5). That's why we are told that people can be "transformed by the renewing of their minds" (Rom. 12:2). That's also why Alcoholics Anonymous talks a lot about correcting "stinkin' thinkin'" to bring about change.

In the blank next to *second base,* write the word *feelings.* It is no secret that what you think about has a lot to do with how you will feel a few minutes later. If you focus your thoughts on a subject, pretty soon you will experience the feelings that are associated with that subject. In counseling, a man once said, "The more I thought about that, the madder I got!" That's the way it works. If you want to feel differently, a good start is thinking differently.

In the blank next to *third base,* write the word *self-talk.* This represents your internal dialogue, i.e., what you say to yourself. You are constantly talking to yourself—sometimes out loud! Sometimes you argue with yourself as you process ideas, as though one part of you is at odds with another part of you. Everyone does this constantly; although, most people are not consciously aware of these internal conversations and the fact that they usually lead to some action or behavioral conclusion.

In the blank next to *home base,* write the word *behavior.* This base represents some action you are going to engage in as a result of running the other bases. This is a simple but effective way of explaining a lot of human behavior, including that of your inner child.

Example BD-2

Let's follow the story of the angry fellow I mentioned earlier. His boss had just chewed him out for something that was not his fault. He managed to control himself and basically responded, "Yes, sir. I'll see that it doesn't happen again." Later, however, he began to think about the situation and noticed his anger increasing. *(He just rounded first base.)* Then, as he put it, "The more I thought about it, the madder I got!" *(He just slid into second base!)* As his anger increased, he wanted to slug his boss. Instead, he reminded himself that that would not be wise. *(He's now breaking for third!)* He began to argue with himself about whether or not he would punch the boss's lights out *(self-talk).* He finally decided not to but slammed his fist on a desk instead. *(He's trying to steal home!)* After work, on the way home, he found himself honking excessively at a driver who abruptly changed lanes in front of him. He then sped up to catch the driver and flash an obscene gesture. This was observed by a policeman, who stopped him and gave him a ticket. *(He gets tagged out, as he reaches home plate!)*

This is obviously a *negative example,* showing how the four-base sequence can lead to *bad behavior* and an undesirable outcome.

Example BD-3

Using the work scenario again, let's follow a *positive example,* in which some *good behavior* results from "running the bases."

Triggering Event (Positive Experience)	Boss comes by, compliments the employee and says he is recommending him for a raise.
Resulting Thoughts (First Base)	"He actually noticed that I worked hard, did a good job. I think he likes me."
Emerging Feelings (Second Base)	Employee feels appreciated, encouraged, motivated, glad he works there.
Internal Self-talk (Third Base)	"Well, I guess my hard work is finally paying off! But then I wonder if he really meant it. Yes, he probably did. There may be a future for me with this company after all!"
Resulting Behavior (Home Base)(Safe!)	Employee smiles more, is friendlier to other workers, willingly stays at work overtime to finish a project.

Transitional Statement: Analyze the difference between thoughts and feelings (emotions). Many people have never consciously considered the difference, but thoughts and feelings are definitely not the same thing. Thoughts are actually generated in a different part of the brain than feelings. "What do you think about that?" is actually a different question from "How do you feel about that?" This differentiation is basic to understanding and applying the Baseball Diamond Model.

Notice that this model gives you a simple diagram for understanding a lot of human behavior. It also identifies four places (bases) at which you can intervene, influence, manage, or even foster change in a person's habit patterns or internal programming. There is more to the Baseball Diamond Model that we would include if we were using it in counseling to bring about therapeutic change. For the purposes of this chapter, however, the information expressed above is enough to give you some significant help in managing your inner child.

Simply put, after some *triggering event* occurs, the following sequence unfolds:

Thoughts → Feelings → Self-talk → Behavior

Example BD-4

Assume that this is the *triggering event* that gets your attention: Pretend that you are in an airport waiting to board your plane. Nearby there is a little girl, about four years old, who is with her parents, who appear to be in their mid-twenties. The little girl is playing around excitedly. A huge airplane lands and taxis toward their gate. The little girl sees it, jumps up, claps, and accidentally knocks over a cup of water belonging to another passenger.

Her father jumps up, screams at her, calls her "stupid," yanks her up by one arm, gives her a swat, deposits her roughly in a seat, and yells, "Now, don't you move!" The little girl begins to sob rather loudly. The dad then yells, "And stop that crying, or I'll give you something to cry about!" The mother sits quietly where she is and does nothing.

In the space below, write some of the thoughts that might go through your mind as you see and hear this triggering event. *(Write your thoughts, not your feelings!)*

_____

_____

_____

_____

Since your thoughts affect your feelings, consider what feelings or emotions might follow the thoughts you wrote above. In the space below, describe some of the feelings or emotions you might be experiencing at that time.

_____

_____

_____

_____

Assume that you actually felt the way you described above. You would likely begin to have a conversation with yourself about the matter. This internal dialogue is called *self-talk* and usually brings a person to some decision regarding what he or she will do (or not do) about a situation. Sentences of self-talk often begin with the words shown below. Complete some of the following sentence fragments to illustrate some of the self-talk that might flow through your mind as you interact (and maybe argue) with yourself. This kind of inner consideration of options and consequences represents *third base* in the analogy:

_____

_____

_____

_____

I really think …

_____

_____

I really feel …

_____

_____

I wonder …

_____

_____

I wonder …

_____

_____

I guess …

_____

_____

I guess …

_____

_____

But then, on the other hand …

_____

_____

Or maybe …

_____

_____

But what if …

_____

_____

If only …

_____

_____

I probably …

_____

_____

Or I could …

_____

_____

But ...

_____

_____

Think it over; what are my options?

_____

_____

_____

_____

OK, I've got to make a decision and come to some conclusion...

_____

_____

_____

_____

Finally, *Home Base* represents some *behavior,* that is the result of the process. Conclude this exercise by describing some behavior that might occur because you went through each step of the process exactly as you described it. *(NOTE: if you decide to do nothing, that is still considered to be the resulting behavior of your self-talk.)*

Resulting behavior:

_____

_____

_____

_____

In summary, the Baseball Diamond Model offers you four points of opportunity to foster change. Any or all of these four points may be used to influence or intervene in the habit patterns (internal programming) of an individual. Worded more specifically for the purposes of this chapter, this model offers four points of consideration to assist you in designing your strategy for managing your inner child.

For the purposes of this chapter, the easiest point of intervention is probably at *third base,* the point of *self-talk.* If you can recognize your inner child's negative, inaccurate, or self-defeating internal dialogue, you can rather easily replace it with self-talk that is positive, accurate, encouraging, and motivating. You may do so by applying the material and the process that are presented in Chapter 14 of this workbook. That entire chapter is dedicated to the dynamics of replacing negative, internal messages with positive, internal messages.

It is up to you and your inner child, however, which of the four points of intervention seem more workable or appropriate for you to use. Although you may eventually use all four of the points in some way, put a checkmark in one of the blanks below to indicate the point (or "base") that you will most likely use first in your management strategy.

___Thought process (correcting negative or obsessive thinking)

___Feelings or emotions (dealing better with anger, fears, etc.)

___Self-talk (improving internal dialogue)

___Behavior (revising or modifying actions directly)

Put an *X* by the one which you are least likely to use.

Raise your level of relationship on the G-Scale Hierarchy of Importance.

In Chapter 5 of Volume 1, we introduced the G-Scale Hierarchy of Importance. We explained that it is normally used to define or assess the level of a relationship between individuals. We mentioned that it has often been a usable tool to help two people see where their relationship is compared to where they would like for it to be on the scale. In this workbook, however, we are applying it to you (the adult) to assess the attitude you have toward yourself as a child.

In other words, we used the scale to determine how you viewed and related to your inner child at that point in the process of reparenting. We acknowledged that one of your major goals would be to raise the level of your relationship with your inner child to a higher level and, ultimately, to the highest level on the G-Scale. It was also noted that if you were not yet able to do this, you may postpone it and deal with it again in a later chapter.

That later chapter was Chapter 12 of this volume. In that chapter, you addressed once again the task of assessing the level of your relationship with your inner child. That time you were also asked to design a strategy for raising your attitude toward the child to a higher level on the scale. In fact, you were challenged to do this with the intention of progressively raising your level on the G-Scale, until that relationship is ultimately characterized by love, the absolute highest level on the scale.

You were given the **ABCs** of achieving such a positive attitude shift, including an acrostic for setting or resetting your affection, based on Colossians 3:2. It is likely, however, that many readers have not yet achieved the level of genuine *agape* love or have not been able to sustain it on a consistent basis. If such is your case, another trip through Chapter 12 would be helpful.

The matter of raising your level of relationship on the G-Scale Hierarchy is included here, however, for the following reasons:

1. You are actually not finished with the process of reparenting until you have reached the top level of the Scale in your relationship with your inner child. In some cases, this requires some additional trips through Chapters 5 and 12 of this workbook.

2. The higher your relationship is on the G-Scale, the easier it will be to manage your inner child.

3. The same methods or techniques that helped you raise your level on the G-Scale will help you manage or parent your inner child more effectively, which is the main purpose of this chapter.

Take a few moments now to "graze" through Chapter 12, for the specific purpose of considering how the content of that chapter might be helpful to you as you design your strategy for managing and parenting your inner child. Use the space below to write some notes regarding any such ideas that come to your mind as you review Chapter 12. A few examples may help you get started:

1. When I completed Chapter 12, my attitude toward my inner child was at the level of on the G-Scale Hierarchy of Importance.

_____

_____

_____

_____

2. I would like to improve my relationship with my inner child by raising it to the level of on the scale.

_____

_____

_____

_____

3. When I reviewed the **ABCs** of achieving such an attitude shift, the following thought or idea seemed important to remember as I design my strategy for managing my inner child:

_____

_____

_____

_____

4. When I reviewed the biblical acrostic for setting or resetting my affection, the following thought or idea seemed important to remember as I design my strategy for managing my inner child:

_____

_____

_____

_____

5. The method(s) of communication (from Chapter 11) that seemed to work pretty well for me in Chapter 12 activities was/were:

_____

_____

_____

_____

6. Add anything else from Chapter 12 that you might want to remember as you design your management strategy.

_____

_____

_____

_____

Taking It Personally

Examine the factors you have explored so far in this chapter.

The reason for examining these factors at this point is to pull together your thoughts and reactions as you prepare to form the strategy uniquely and specifically designed for your little child within.

Glance back through each of the subsections listed below (from this chapter), and write down any ideas or conclusions you will want to remember and consider as you assume your role as _chief strategy architect and programming designer extraordinaire_! (In other words, make a few notes…) Titles of subsections follow:

1. Explain why good parenting requires managing the child.

_____

_____

_____

_____

2. X-clude (or "X-out") some myths about parenting.

_____

_____

_____

_____

3. Pay attention to the uniqueness of your inner child.

_____

_____

_____

_____

4. Learn the management style that will work best for you.

_____

_____

_____

_____

5. Observe and apply the principles of the Baseball Diamond Model.

_____

_____

_____

_____

6. Raise your level of relationship on the G-Scale Hierarchy of Importance.

_____

_____

_____

_____

7. If there are any additional thoughts, ideas, or cautions you would like to remember as you decide on the actual wording of your strategy, include them here:

_____

_____

_____

_____

Application

You are now *almost* ready to form the actual statement of your strategy!

Before you begin to choose your words and organize your sentences, read through the Sample Statement of Strategy that follows. It will show you how John used the information from this chapter to compose his personal Statement of Strategy. He considered his responses to all the exercises as well as the reminders he wrote in his notes in the section you just completed. He wrote and re-wrote some of the sentences until he was satisfied that the following statement was (and still is) well-suited for him and his inner child.

Sample Statement of Strategy

(Based on John's Use of Information from This Chapter)

Reparenting requires me (the adult) to "manage" my inner child. This is an ongoing process that will continue throughout my life. In order to do this effectively, I must decide on the kind of experience and the style of relationship I will use to manage, guide, and continue to nurture my inner child.

In managing my inner child, I need to use some principles of good parenting. I will remember that withholding attention or affection from me did not work very well when my parents tried it. I will also remember that warm, kind words seemed to bring out the best in me when I was a child.

I will commit to pay attention to the uniqueness of my inner child. I think one of his spiritual gifts is discernment, which may make him more sensitive than most other children. He seems to be passionate about helping other people. I need to help him set and keep good boundaries, so he can become less co-dependent and less of an enabler. He has musical abilities. I will help him enjoy performing for the right reasons and not get too hooked into seeking the approval (or applause) of others. His primary temperament appears to be sanguine, and his secondary seems to be melancholy, so I will make myself aware of the strengths, the weaknesses, and the legitimate needs of that combination. This will help me to understand him and interact in a way that calms some of his fears and brings out the best in him. I will consider his life experiences at impressionable times and how these have affected him. For example, he did not see his father during most of four impressionable years, from the time he started first grade until he entered fourth grade. This has resulted in some symptoms of the father deficit, and it can cause him to seek too hard for the approval of coaches, male teachers, and other male role models. I will take this into consideration, along with the other factors that make up his S-H-A-P-E.

As I considered the different management styles, the one that seems most appropriate for "Little John" is to handle or treat him with care. I will remember that harshness drives him away and shuts him down. When it is necessary to switch to a secondary style of management, the setting of limits or parameters is probably the next best approach. I will remember that angry demands, over-reactions, and physical roughness feed his fears and are interpreted by him as rejection and threat of abandonment.

From the Baseball Diamond Model I learned several ways I could go about changing some of the childish behavior that shows up now and then. The one that will probably work best with "Little John" is to improve his self-talk. I know of things that he sometimes says to himself that make him feel worse and then act out in certain ways. I think I can help him replace some of the old, negative self-talk with new and better, positive self-talk. I know that the best way to deal with a bad habit is to replace it with a good habit. I will work on this by using some of the communication methods I learned in Chapter 13, especially opposite hand-written conversation and creative expression (with the adult participating).

When I started the reparenting process, our relationship was at the level of tolerance. I have managed to raise it to acceptance. I promise to continue working until I have raised it to the level of *agape* love. Then I will be able to care for him (and myself) with unconditional, positive regard, like God does.

I admit that I do not yet know what all of this will look like when I figure out how to apply it on a day to day basis. I will re-read this statement of strategy from time to time, however, in order to keep my perspective and hopefully get better and better at managing The Kid as we continue our journey of reparenting."

Guess what? YOU ARE FINALLY READY!

Using the information from this chapter, your responses to the exercises, the reminders you have written in your notes above, and the Sample Statement of Strategy as a guide, *start the countdown*! Ten …

9. Look at the space provided for you to compose your actual statement of strategy. Write in the title, "My Personal Statement of Strategy for Managing My Inner Child."

8. Use the same opening paragraph that John used in the Sample Statement of Strategy. It is an excellent introductory statement, and it clearly and accurately defines your task. Write it word for word.

7. Use John's first sentence from the second paragraph of the sample. Complete your second paragraph with two or three things you will want to remember about good parenting.

6. Start your third paragraph with John's lead sentence for that paragraph. The rest of paragraph three should include references to and consideration of the unique S-H-A-P-E of your own child within.

5. The fourth paragraph should designate the management style that you believe will work best with your inner child, the one that probably would work at times when the first one doesn't, and anything else you will want to remember about using these styles.

4. The fifth paragraph should state something (or some things) you learned from the Baseball Diamond Model and how you plan to apply it/them.

3. Let paragraph six refer to your level of relationship on the G-Scale Hierarchy of Importance when you began the reparenting process, where it is now, and your commitment in that regard for the future.

2. Use the seventh paragraph to state any additional thoughts, ideas, or cautions you would like to remember.

1. Use the final paragraph to "wrap-up" and "sign-off." In other words, attempt to conclude your strategy with a sentence or two that brings it in for an impressive landing! For this, feel free to wax briefly eloquent; add a dab of fleeting, fragrant philosophy; or sprinkle a dash of aromatic, inspirational departure!

Go!

The space below is provided for you to write out your actual statement of strategy. Do not use it, however, until you have composed, re-read, revised, edited, and are satisfied that your final draft is well-suited for you and your inner child. So, get some blank paper, and get started!

Begin by writing the title as instructed in item 9 above (centered left and right). Then copy the first paragraph as instructed in item 8 above. Continue to compose your remaining seven paragraphs according to the guidelines and suggestions above. When you have finished the first draft, re-read, think, pray, and make whatever changes you feel are appropriate.

If you are using this workbook in counseling, in a group, or under the guidance of some person of accountability, it would be in order to share your composition and consider their input, if you wish. Do this before you copy your final draft into the workbook, in case you decide to change or add something.

Finally, copy your final, final, final draft into the space provided below!

_____

_____

_____

_____

_____

_____

_____

_____

_____

_____

_____

Little Mona Did It

When I found out that I was pregnant with my daughter, Mary, I had visions of a happy, cooing baby that smelled good all the time. I didn't fantasize about dirty diapers, 2:00 a.m. feedings, and colic. I knew about those things, but as with most parents, my dreams and expectations did not exactly match the reality that unfolded—at least, not all the time. But still I loved her!

When it came to my inner child, my expectations were just as unrealistic. I had wonderful friends who seemed to love that little girl, but I found it really hard to love that crying, demanding, little child inside. She cried relentlessly, "Feed me, love me. I feel empty. I feel abused!" Sometimes it seemed that there was not enough love in this whole world to fill that deep and constant need.

At times, I tried to somehow drown her out. Like one day when there was a shooting at a train station. That same day, there was a lady who committed suicide. Both of these stories were on the news that night, and The Kid panicked. She did that when events were scary and out of her control. I could not calm her down or drown her out. Finally, we fell asleep exhausted, but the deep and terrifying night continued.

She dreamed she was the one with the gun, the one in control. But having that much power terrified her even more. In the dream, she began to fire the gun, shooting at everything and everyone who had ever hurt her. She woke up startled, still terrified, and very angry.

The next day, she yelled at me and Dr. G. and others. She even yelled at herself! She texted angry messages. She was out of control, like a child throwing a tantrum. That's when I realized that what she needed was someone bigger and wiser and stronger to stop her and to hold her until she settled down, felt secure, and got back in control. In other words, that situation made it necessary for me to manage and to parent Little Mona. I must have reached way down and drawn from strength I didn't know I had, but with God's help, I did it! And we survived!

I must admit that parenting my inner child is much harder than parenting my outer one! I can see Mary. She talks to me in clear English and tells me what she wants, feels, and needs. I can reason with her and can actually drown her out sometimes, if I need to! Yes, it is definitely harder for me to listen to, understand, reason with, and manage my inner child, my inner heart.

Parenting my outer child was a learning process, and so is parenting the child within. I am still learning the necessary skills, but I'm getting better all the time! And so can you!

I'll close by telling you what I often tell myself: "It will be so worth it! Just don't weaken!"

Chapter 16

Improving and Applying Relationship Skills

Vantage Point

A LADY WALKED into my counseling office for her first counseling appointment. Her first words to me were a question. Before she even sat down, she asked, "Is there a sign on my back that says, 'Abuse me!'?"

I answered, "I don't see one. Why do you ask?"

She said, "Because every relationship I get into turns out that way. I get abused. Male or female, if I get close, I end up getting abused in some way."

Toward the end of our third session, I said to her, "Now I know the answer to your original question. You might as well have a sign on your back that says, 'Abuse me!' The truth is, you not only invite people to abuse you, you almost require it. It's like that's the only way you know how to relate to people—especially to members of the opposite sex."

Behind all of this was the way she viewed herself. She might as well also have worn a sign that said, "I am a victim," because that was her primary identity. So imagine with me this lady wearing one of those big a-frame signs that people sometimes wear as they walk around advertising a new product or a special event. In front, the sign says, "I am a victim," and in back it says, "Abuse me!"

This reminds me of the cartoon I saw in a magazine. A man had stopped directly under a bird perched on a limb. He looked up and said to the bird, "Go ahead, everybody else does!" (In case you didn't catch this, ask somebody what the man expected the bird to do on him.)

All of this does not justify or excuse the fact that people abused the lady. It simply explains it, or at least a lot of it. The point is that we really do teach people how to treat us. Not completely, but to a large extent, we telegraph in various ways how we view ourselves and the ways we expect others to treat us. Many people seem more than willing to accept our invitations and accommodate our expectations, especially if it somehow feeds their pride, elevates their prestige, or gives them some kind of sordid pleasure.

The key factors we considered in this lady's therapy were as follows: (1) identity, (2) self-image, (3) temperament, and (4) personality. When these four elements were corrected and became healthy, so did her relationships. Eventually, she was able to change the message on both sides of the metaphorical sign she was wearing! She was then ready (and able!) to develop good relationship skills, including healthy boundaries.

In this chapter, we will consider the same four elements mentioned above. We will then apply them for the distinct purpose of improving that unique, personal, and vital relationship between you (the adult) and your inner child. That is an important re-parenting goal and is the reason this chapter has been included.

From the four factors mentioned above, the following seven questions emerge:

1. How do I presently define my identity?
2. What is my true identity, and how do I attain it?
3. What factors determine my self-image?
4. How do I go about improving my self-image?
5. What is the difference in temperament and personality?
6. What do temperament and personality factors have to do with my relationship skills?
7. How can I improve my relationship skills and apply them to my process of re-parenting?

Contrary to popular belief, knowing the questions is a major point of progress toward finding and learning the answers. Ready, set, go

Input from Dr. G.

Question 1: How do I presently define my identity?

Kathryn attended a group I led on "Grieving Life Losses." As people introduced themselves, they were asked to tell their names and something about themselves that would explain their reasons for attending that group. When Kathryn's turn came, she gave her name and said, "I am a victim of 9-11-01. I was in one of the Twin Towers when the terrorists crashed the planes into the buildings." The other members of the group reacted with interest and compassion. They wanted to hear more. The introductory process stopped for several minutes while she answered questions and basically told her story.

That was OK—actually understandable—even though it was happening almost two years after the incident. The problem was that in sessions two, three, and four, she also found opportunities to identify herself in the same way, refer again to her experience, and dominate more than her share of the time. When I, as group leader, began to impose a little structure to foster more balance of interaction, she became visibly upset. When the group began trying to help her move past the tragedy of 9-11-01, she stopped coming altogether. I contacted her personally, and she said that the group was no longer helpful because they had lost interest in her and her issues. She said that the same thing had happened with other groups she had attended.

It was obvious that her primary identity was "victim of 9-11-01." That had become her claim to fame. She received attention and other emotional payoffs from people when she told her story. It was as though she could not risk losing that identity for fear that there would be no person of significance left. Although she had a few other adult roles, she apparently lacked personal definition apart from her association with that infamous event of 2001.

People may derive their personal definitions or primary identities (positive or negative) from a variety of sources. Some of those sources are listed below. Feel free to add a tenth category by the word *other,* if you wish.

1. A famous or impactful event or experience
2. Physical appearance or characteristics— good or bad— height, hair color, etc.
3. Career, skills, achievements, or outstanding abilities
4. "Roots," ethnicity, nationality, family of origin, etc.
5. Association with celebrities, special friends, or acquaintances
6. Affiliations, i.e., prestigious churches, companies, schools, clubs, etc.
7. Religious convictions, spirituality, relationship with God
8. Influence or opinions of significant others, including abusers
9. Adult roles, titles, labels, or credentials
10. Other:_____

Just off the top of your head, which two or three of the sources above do you think probably have the greatest influence on your primary identity? Another way of asking the same thing is: Which two or three of those sources seem to give you the best answer to the question, "Who am I?"

_____

_____

_____

_____

Now let's see if we can "zero in" a little more on your primary source(s) of identity. We will do this by considering three aspects of your personal definition.

1. Your Private Self: The You No One Sees

Look at the sentences below. Complete each of them by writing the first thing that comes to your mind. Avoid listing physical characteristics, like height, hair color, or appearance. Instead, write what you are like inside.

Here are some examples of what others have written:

- I am someone who *isn't sure who I really am.*
- I am someone who *cares too much what people think.*
- I am someone who *hides my true feelings most of the time.*
- I am someone who *often feels more afraid than I seem.*
- I am someone who *is probably too sensitive.*
- I am someone who *wants to be a better person.*
- I am someone who *wonders a lot about life.*
- I am someone who *was abused as a child.*

Now it's your turn. Include positive and/or negative responses. Complete all eight sentences.

1. I am someone who _____.

2. I am someone who _____.

3. I am someone who _____.

4. I am someone who _____.

5. I am someone who _____.

6. I am someone who _____.

7. I am someone who _____.

8. I am someone who _____.

How did that feel? Any problems doing it? Any surprises or interesting thoughts as you looked back over what you wrote? Respond below.

_____

_____

_____

_____

2. The Mug Shot on Your I.D.: The You That People See

Once again, finish the following sentences with the first thing that pops into your mind, excluding physical characteristics.

Here are some examples of what others have written:

- Others see me as someone who *is willing to take chances.*
- Others see me as someone who *sometimes loses my temper.*
- Others see me as someone who *likes to help people.*
- Others see me as someone who *is usually easy to get along with.*
- Others see me as someone who *is sort of a loner.*
- Others see me as someone who *is more serious than I really am.*
- Others see me as someone who *has it all together.*
- Others see me as someone who *lives a pretty good Christian life.*

Now it's your turn again. Include positive and/or negative responses. Complete all eight sentences.

1. Others see me as someone who _____ .

2. Others see me as someone who _____ .

3. Others see me as someone who _____ .

4. Others see me as someone who _____ .

5. Others see me as someone who _____ .

6. Others see me as someone who _____ .

7. Others see me as someone who _____ .

8. Others see me as someone who _____ .

How did that feel? Any problems doing it? Any surprises or interesting thoughts as you looked back over what you wrote? Respond below.

_____

_____

_____

_____

3. Your Charades and Masquerades: The Adult Roles and Labels You Wear

Think of several labels or titles that adults may wear, i.e., labels or titles by which adults may introduce themselves or identify themselves. These may include immediate family roles, extended family relationships, occupations or career titles, other skills you have developed, positions in organizations, hobbies, special interests, recreation or sports involvement, social relationships, and other areas of your life. A few specific examples may include father, mother, in-law, teacher, carpenter, guitar player, painter, baby-sitter, computer programmer, internet buff, baseball fan, crafts person, fishing buddy, bridge partner, gourmet cook, bargain shopper, and many others.

List below eight or more adult labels that apply to you:

1. _____   2. _____

3. _____   4. _____

5. _____   6. _____

7. _____   8. _____

9. _____   10. _____

Now, look back over the roles and labels that you wrote in the blanks. Think about how each of them impacts or affects your life. Imagine how different your life would be without each of them. Pick two or three of them that you could omit without missing them much or grieving a loss. Cross out the numbers of these two or three that you could rather easily do without. (It might even be a relief to drop some of them!)

Continue to identify additional adult roles and labels on your list to which you are not very emotionally attached. One at a time, cross out the ones that are least important to you, until only three are left. The three remaining should be the ones to which you relate most strongly.

List the remaining three below in the order of emotional importance to you. Let number one represent the role or label that would leave the greatest vacuum or vacancy if it were suddenly eliminated from your life. List numbers two and three according to the same criteria. These three roles, titles, or labels are the ones most likely to be associated with your basic identity.

We are still trying to "zero in" on your primary source(s) of identity. We are trying to find your best answer to the question, "Who am I?"

1. Look over what you wrote to complete the sentences under "Your Private Self: The You No One Sees." Do any of those responses give you a clue about your primary or secondary identity? If so, write the clue or insight below.

_____

_____

_____

_____

2. Look over what you wrote to complete the sentences under "The Mug Shot On Your I.D.: The You People See." Do any of those responses give you a clue about your primary or secondary identity? If so, write the clue or insight below.

_____

_____

_____

_____

3. Look over the three adult roles, titles, or labels you selected as having the most emotional importance to you under "Your Charades and Masquerades: The Adult Roles and Labels You Wear." Do any of those responses give you a clue about your primary or secondary identity? If so, write the clue or insight below.

_____

_____

_____

_____

4. Now you should be able to "zero in" on your best answers to the question, "Who am I?" according to your present belief system. Do this by completing the following sentences:

   Most of all, I am _____.

   I am also _____.

5. Discuss how you feel about what you wrote above. Are you satisfied with your responses? Do they seem to be true and sincere expressions of how you presently define your identity? Explain below.

_____

_____

_____

_____

Question 2: What is my true identity, and how do I attain it?

The true identity of every believer is clearly stated in Scripture. For all who have placed their faith in Jesus Christ as their Savior, the following Scripture references express their true identity as children of God:

I am deeply loved.

By this the love of God was manifested in us, that God has sent His only begotten Son into the world so that we might live through Him. In this is love, not that we loved God, but that He loved us and sent his Son to be the propitiation for our sins. Beloved, if God so loved us, we also ought to love one another.

—1 John 4:9–11

I am fully pleasing.

Therefore having been justified by faith we have the peace with God through our Lord, Jesus Christ.

—Romans 5:1

I am fully accepted.

And although you were formerly alienated and hostile in mind, engaged in evil deeds, yet He has now reconciled you in His fleshly body through death, in order to present you before Him holy and blameless and beyond reproach …

—Colossians 1:21–22

I am a new creation.

Therefore, if anyone is in Christ, he is a new creation; old things have passed away; behold, all things have become new.

—2 Corinthians 5:17

I am complete in Christ.

… and in Him you have been made complete, and He is the head over all rule and authority …
—Colossians 2:10

There is a Declaration I have been using with clients for years. I did not compose it, and I honestly do not remember where I got it, but it expresses the heart of these verses in a way that has helped many people to understand their true identity from God's perspective. I suggest that you first read it silently to get a feel for what it says. Then read it aloud to claim and declare your true identity in Christ.

Declaration

Because of Christ's redemption,
I am a new creation of infinite worth.
I am deeply loved,
I am completely forgiven,
I am fully pleasing,
I am totally accepted by God.
I am absolutely complete in Christ.

When my performance
reflects my new identity in Christ,
that reflection is dynamically unique.

There has never been another person like me
in the history of mankind,
nor will there ever be.
God has made an original,
one of a kind, a special person.

Some people have difficulty getting themselves to actually read the Declaration aloud. This may be because they don't believe that there is any real benefit from doing it. If you are one of those people, let me remind you that there is much power of persuasion in what you hear yourself say. This is one application of Romans 10:17, "Faith comes by hearing ..." Romans 10:9–10 also confirms the principle that what we confess with our mouths becomes a "done deal" in our hearts. Once again, therefore, I would urge you to speak the Declaration aloud, ideally, every day for a couple of weeks! "Death and life are in the power of the tongue ..." (Proverbs 18:21). In this case, it is life.

Your next step in attaining or realizing your true identity as a child of God is examining the following "I am" statements from Scripture. Read all the way through them, considering what each verse says about "who you are." (Some of them will be harder for you to believe than others.)

1. I am God's child, for I am born again of the incorruptible seed of the Word of God, which lives and abides forever (1 Peter 1:23).
2. I am forgiven of all my sins and washed in the blood (Ephesians 1:7).
3. I am a new creation in Christ (2 Corinthians 5:17).
4. I am acceptable and accepted in Christ (Ephesians 1:6).
5. I am delivered from the power of darkness and transformed into God's kingdom (Colossians 1:13).

6. I am blessed (Deuteronomy 28:2–14).

7. I am redeemed from the curse of the law (Galatians 3:13).

8. I am strong in the Lord (Ephesians 6:10).

9. I am chosen and beloved of God (1 Thessalonians 1:4).

10. I am called to be a saint (Romans 1:7).

11. I am the apple of my Father's eye (Psalm 17:80).

12. I am a joint heir with Christ (Romans 8:17).

13. I am qualified to share in His inheritance (Colossians 1:12).

14. I am guaranteed a part in His inheritance (Ephesians 1:14).

15. I am His workmanship, created in Christ for good works (Ephesians 2:10).

16. I am one of many brothers and sisters in Christ's family (Romans 8:29).

17. I am given access to the mind of Christ (1 Corinthians 2:16).

18. I am reconciled with God (2 Corinthians 5:18).

19. I am able to approach the heavenly Father in prayer at any time (Matthew 6:6–9).

20. I am a king and a priest unto God (Revelation 1:6).

21. I am the temple of the Holy Spirit (1 Corinthians 6:19).

22. I am the head and not the tail (Deuteronomy 28:13).

23. I am a partaker of His divine nature (2 Peter 1:4).

24. I am the righteousness of God in Christ (2 Corinthians 5:21).

25. I am gradually being changed into His image (Philippians 1:6).

26. I am more than a conqueror through Christ (Romans 8:37).

27. I am eternally secure in the love of God (Romans 8:35–39).

28. I am promised a place with Him in heaven forever (John 14:2–3).

29. I am a member of the household of God (Ephesians 2:19).

30. I am assured that I will dwell in the Lord's house forever (Psalm 23:6).

Now that you have read and examined all thirty of the "I am" statements above, ask yourself this question: "Which of these statements do I really believe and accept without question?" Each time you find one that you can accept at face value in regard to your true identity as a child of God, circle the numeral to the left of the statement.

If you could not circle all of the items, remind yourself that these statements came directly from Holy Scripture, which we are instructed to accept as the inspired Word of God. ("All Scripture is given by inspiration of God ..." [2 Timothy 3:16].) Next, take a moment to pray, asking the Lord to give you the understanding, grace, and faith to accept, receive, and realize your true identity in Christ. Then, see if there are any additional statements that you can claim and circle on the basis of increased faith.

Finally, if there are still some statements you have not circled, identify a few of them that seem right to you theologically but, for some reason, they are hard for you to apply to yourself. In other words, you can accept and believe these statements for certain other people, but they do not seem to be true for you. Put check marks by a few of these that seem most important to you. Then actually get a Bible, look up the scriptures, and read them aloud to yourself. ("Faith cometh by hearing, and hearing by the Word of God" [Romans 10:17].) Hopefully, you will be able eventually to claim and circle the rest of the statements regarding your true identity in Christ.

To complete this exercise, think of a t-shirt that might display an accurate representation of your true identity. People wear a lot of t-shirts with words, symbols, logos, or pictures on them. Most of the time, they have chosen to wear a certain t-shirt in order to make some kind of a statement about themselves. They are obviously willing to be identified with the message on the shirt, or they would refuse to wear it in public.

With this in mind, design a couple of t-shirts that you would be willing to wear in public. You may use words, symbols, logos, or pictures, but whatever you choose to print or draw on the shirts must be accurate representations of some significant aspects of your true identity.

T-SHIRT NO. 1

Front   Back

T-SHIRT NO. 2

Front   Back

Glance back over this section. Then respond to the following questions: Do you feel that you have a pretty good understanding of your true identity? Do you feel that you have pretty well accepted and attained your true identity, or do you still have a long way to go? What is something you learned in this section that may help you continue to make progress? Are there some unanswered questions that still have you a little puzzled about your true identity? If so, try to express them or discuss them below.

_____

_____

_____

_____

Question 3: What factors determine my self-image?

First, let me clarify what we mean by self-image in this workbook. It is the image that you project to yourself, inside yourself, about yourself. It is of utmost importance because this image, projected onto the monitor of your mind, is the reality you respond to about yourself. Whether it is right or wrong, true or false, accurate or inaccurate, it is still the reality to which you respond and in which you operate. The extreme importance of your self-image can hardly be over-emphasized. It is an extension of your belief system, and therefore it *is* reality to you!

Your self-image is determined by three factors. Think of it like a three-legged stool on which you are trying to stand in order to change a light bulb. Imagine the difficulty you would have if each leg of the stool were a different length. It would be unstable, to say the least, and very difficult to keep balanced! The same principle applies to your self-image: instability and lack of emotional balance may telegraph a faulty self-image!

Using the three-legged stool analogy once again, imagine yourself trying to use such a stool effectively if one of its legs is missing completely! This, of course, would be impossible, which once again points out the tremendous importance of all three factors being present, healthy, available, and functional.

Your next assignment, therefore, is to study the chart entitled *Self-Image Factors*. Notice the three factors in the center of the page. Next, study the column on the right side of the chart. That side of the chart reveals the ways you will tend to feel if the three factors are healthy and available. Then, focus on the left side of the chart. This is a little more complicated, but basically, it describes the ways you will tend to feel if any of your three factors are deficit, unhealthy, or unavailable.

Usually, it is easier to identify your deficits from the left side of the chart. Notice which fears are associated with each factor. Then notice whom you will tend to blame if each factor is in need of repair or is lacking in some regard.

Self-Image Factors

NEGATIVE FEELINGS (If factor not developed properly)	FACTORS	POSITIVE FEELINGS (If factor is developed properly)
Rejection, anger, hostility (Blame others, externalize)	**Belongingness**	I am wanted, cared for, accepted, part of a group.

Guilt, "at fault," responsible   **Self-Worth**   I count. I'm OK. I'm
(Blame self, internalize)   important to someone important.

Fears and insecurities   **Competence**   I can achieve, do something
(Blame God, fate, or whoever   well, have hope and confidence.
you believe runs the universe)   I can try things and risk failure.

Using the chart above, attempt to fill in the blanks in the sentences that follow:

1. According to the chart, the three factors that determine your self-image are:

    a. A sense of _____.

    b. A sense of _____.

    c. A sense of _____.

2. If the belongingness factor is healthy and available, you will find it easy to feel _____ and a _____ of a group.

3. If the self-worth factor is healthy and available, you will find it easy to feel _____ to someone who is _____ to you.

4. If the competence factor is healthy and available, you will find it easy to feel:

    a. that you can achieve, do something _____; or

    b. have enough confidence to _____ things and risk _____.

5. If the belongingness factor is unhealthy or unavailable, you will find it easy to feel _____, excluded, and unwanted; and you will tend to blame _____, i.e., to externalize blame.

6. If the self-worth factor is unhealthy or unavailable, you will find it easy to feel too _____ or too personally at fault; and you will tend to blame _____, i.e., to internalize blame.

7. If the competence factor is unhealthy or unavailable, you will find it easy to feel a variety of fears and _____; and you will tend to blame _____, fate, or whoever or whatever you believe "runs the universe."

With this information in mind, do your best to assess the condition of these three factors in your own self-image. Circle a number below to indicate your assessment of each factor. The higher numbers indicate the healthier factors, and the lower numbers indicate the factors with the greatest deficits.

The Belongingness Factor

Deficit, unhealthy,   Adequate, healthy,
  or unavailable   1 2 3 4 5 6 7 8 9   and available

The Self-worth Factor

Deficit, unhealthy,   Adequate, healthy,
  or unavailable   1 2 3 4 5 6 7 8 9   and available

The Competence Factor

Deficit, unhealthy,   Adequate, healthy,
  or unavailable   1 2 3 4 5 6 7 8 9   and available

Look at your assessment of each factor, and then use the space below to write a summary statement regarding the present condition of your self-image overall. What does this seem to reveal about your attitude toward yourself?

_____

_____

_____

_____

Question 4: How do I go about improving my self-image?

To improve your self-image, you must take seriously the assessment you made in Question 3 above. Think of the analogy of the three-legged stool, and make a decision to attain the emotional balance and stability that are necessary ingredients for good relationship skills. Take a moment to remind yourself of the title of this chapter, and you'll be ready to press on!

Next, get ready for three profound principles:

1. Each of the three factors comes more from one particular significant other than from anyone (or everyone) else! You may need to read that another time or two.

   Actually, it is rather simple in its application. It is simply referring to the fact that *usually and traditionally:*

   a. Your sense of *belongingness* comes more from your *dad* (or a father figure) than from any other individual.

   b. Your sense of *competence* comes more from your *mom* (or a mother figure) than from any other individual.

   c. Your sense of *self-worth comes more from someone other than mom or dad,* who is very important to you! This *someone other than* mom or dad is called a "Big Brother Type." It is often an actual big brother, but it does not have to be. In my case, I do not have a big brother. I *am* the big brother; but I had a red-headed aunt who was a few years older than I and who was around a lot when I was eight, nine, and ten years old … and she performed this important role for me! She made me feel *important* to someone who was *important* to me, other than mom and dad, and thereby made a significant contribution to my sense of self-worth.

   The psychology behind this is that there comes the time when a child asks this question: "Is there anyone around, outside of mom and dad, who is important and valuable to me, who seems to think that I am also important and valuable?" If so, the child will tend to accept that person's opinion as valid. This person may be a relative, a friend, a neighbor, a baby-sitter, someone from church, someone from school, or someone else who crosses your path at a crucial time of readiness. The point is that this person will leave an indelible impression that either validates or invalidates your sense of self-worth.

   Of course, many people contribute to all of our impressions about ourselves, but almost everyone I have counseled about this could come up with a single, primary contributor or else admit that there was no one. In which case there was a significant vacuum in the factor that was supposed to contain his or her self-worth.

   Can you identify the person who primarily performed this "Big Brother" role in your case? If so, use the space below to comment on this person and if the impression he or she left was positive or negative.

   _____

   _____

_____

_____

2. Nobody had perfect parents, nobody is a perfect parent, and nobody was a perfect child. Therefore, everyone reaches adulthood with certain deficits in his or her self-image factors.

   This is not about parent-bashing. Even if someone could have parents who perfectly represented everything about self-image factors at appropriate developmental stages, that person would not receive and internalize it all because that person would not be a perfect child. It is still a fact, therefore, that everyone who reaches adulthood has some room for improvement of his or her self-image.

3. If/since your primary caretakers failed to provide all the positive input and role-modeling that you needed, you can depend on the Lord to intervene and provide remedially in two ways.

   First, He will bring across your path individuals who will possess personal qualities and characteristics that will correct or complete the work that your primary caretakers were supposed to accomplish in your self-image. Some of these people may be friends, coaches, instructors, work associates, school teachers, Sunday school teachers, mentors, relatives, sweethearts, or ultimately, your husband or wife. You can probably think of a few of these people whose influence has made you a better person. If you can't right now, eventually you will be able to…someday! It is still true that "iron sharpeneth iron" (Proverbs 27:17); although, it may feel more like sandpaper at the time!

   Second, God will personally complete the work, if you will let Him. If you ignore or forget everything else, try to catch this profound principle and cling to it:

   - If your father did not do a very good job of demonstrating fatherlyness, you can bypass the earthly role-model who failed you and go directly to the heavenly Father to correct your father-deficit and complete your sense of belongingness!
   - If your mother did not do a very good job of demonstrating motherlynes, you can bypass the earthly role-model who failed you and go directly to the Holy Spirit, the Mother Hen of Heaven, to complete your sense of competence!
   - If your "big brother type" did not do a very good job of demonstrating "big brotherlyness" (or was not there at all), you can bypass the earthly role-model who failed you and go directly to Jesus, the Firstborn of your heavenly family, your Big Brother forever, to correct your big brother deficit and complete your sense of

self-worth. You are an "heir and joint-heir with Him"! And when you realize that if you had been the only one who ever lived, He would have still died on the cross just for you, your stock goes up instantly and significantly, and your self-worth soars! As it is expressed on the self-image chart, you realize that you are very important to Someone who is very important to you … and that fulfills an accurate sense of your ultimate self-worth!

Take a few moments to think about the three profound principles that you have just finished reading and how they relate to Question 4 above. Use the space that follows to express anything about those three principles that impressed you, surprised you, or raised additional questions about the way a person's self-image can be improved.

_____

_____

_____

_____

Question 5: What is the difference in temperament and personality?

It is my intention to give you the short answer to this question. For our purposes, we do not need to go into the 567 questions of the Minnesota Multiphasic Personality Inventory. Neither do we need to juggle the alphabetical dichotomies of the Myers Briggs Type Indicator to determine which of the sixteen combinations best represents your personality type. Either of these could be interesting and helpful (or alarming!) in its own way, but neither is necessary for your reparenting.

Elsewhere in this workbook, we have referred to temperament as the in-born, God-given cluster of tendencies that determine the way you perceive, interpret, and respond to your environment. In accordance with the explanations presented by doctors. Richard and Phyllis Arno of the National Christian Counselors Association, these tendencies may or may not emerge and develop as God intended, depending on the circumstances and experiences of your life that may have either fostered or inhibited them.

In very abbreviated form, therefore, our working explanation of the difference between temperament and personality is as follows:

1. Think of temperament as the in-born, God-given way you were hard-wired, providing the potential to unfold according to God's plan, purpose, and will for your life.

2. Think of personality as the way in which your potential has, in reality, unfolded and emerged, providing the patterns, preferences, and programming that actually characterize your daily life.

3. Some people consider the two words to mean the same thing, or almost the same thing, and some may use the two words interchangeably. If you will accept the working explanation as I have presented it here, however, it will give you the best platform from which to understand yourself, to improve your relationship skills, and to apply them to your inner child.

4. Remember that all temperament types and all personality types are legitimate, and all types are legitimately different from each other. All types have strengths, and all types have weaknesses, but all types should try to emphasize their strengths and minimize their weaknesses. All types have legitimate needs, and all types have something unique to offer in meeting the needs of others. All types have the ability to become mentally and spiritually healthy, and all types have the capacity to relate personally and intimately with God.

In the paragraph you have just finished reading (item 4 above), I presented some ways in which temperament and personality can be compared or contrasted. Look back over that paragraph, please, and consider which of those observations are most interesting or informative to you. Use the space below to share two or three of the facts that are the most impressive to you.

Question 6: What do temperament and personality factors have to do with my relationship skills?

Which of the following choices would you guess to be the best answer to Question 6?

       a. A lot.   c. Very much.

       b. A whole lot.   d. More than I think.

Guess what? You are right! Regardless of which of the answers you chose, you are likely correct in your opinion that temperament and personality factors are significantly related to your relationship skills—and probably even more so than most people think!

Let's explore how some of these factors may actually guide or govern the way you behave in interpersonal relationships, including your relationships with family, friends, work associates, your inner child, and even God.

I was amused at a series of children's books on certain topics related to science. The first one I saw was entitled *All About Dinosaurs*. Another was entitled *All About Weather*. I laughed out loud when I noticed the one entitled *All About Our Solar System*. The thing that struck me so funny was the fact that none of the books in the "All About Series" was more than a quarter-inch thick! That reminded me of the impossibility of ever saying *everything* about anything, especially in one book! It also brought to mind the fact that choosing what to leave unsaid is probably as important as choosing what to say in a certain context. All this brainwork brought me to the decision to include here only three additional ideas that should help you improve and apply relationship skills more effectively in your reparenting process.

The first is called *inclusion,* and it has to do with the extent to which your inner child needs or desires to be included in interpersonal relationships. A secondary aspect of this is if The Kid prefers for others to approach him or her for socialization or if the child prefers to do the approaching for such inclusion.

The second is called *control,* and it has to do with the extent to which your inner child needs or desires for there to be a clear definition of who holds the power or dominance in a relationship. A secondary aspect of this is whether The Kid prefers for the other party or parties to hold the controlling power or the child prefers to hold the control or dominance in the relationship.

The third is called *affection*, and it has to do with the extent to which your inner child needs or desires to give or receive expressions of love and affection. A secondary aspect of this is whether The Kid prefers for the other party or parties to initiate the expression of affection or the child prefers to do the initiating. If the child prefers for the other person to originate the expression, then your inner child is considered to be more responsive than expressive.

How well do you know your inner child in regard to these three areas of temperament manifestation? Can you see that the unique needs and preferences of your inner child in these three areas can have a lot to do with The Kid's response to your approach, style, and strategy of relating? (These are rhetorical questions and do not require a written response.)

In view of all you have learned about your inner child thus far, as well as all you can remember about yourself as a child, do your best to answer the following questions as they relate to the precious, little person inside you.

1. Regarding *inclusion*:
    a. How strong is the need or desire of your inner child to be involved in interpersonal relationships?
        Very weak   Weak   Moderate   Strong   Very strong

    b. Does The Kid prefer for others to approach him or her for socialization, or does The Kid prefer to do the approaching?

        Usually prefers for   Either way is   Usually prefers to
        others to approach   equally OK.   do the approaching

2. Regarding *control*:
   a. How strong is the need or desire to have a clear definition of who holds the power or dominance in a relationship?

   Very weak   Weak   Moderate   Strong Very strong

   b. Who does The Kid prefer to hold the power or dominance in a relationship?

   Usually prefers for   Either way is   Usually prefers to
   others to approach   equally OK.   do the approaching

3. Regarding *affection*:
   a. How strong is the need or desire to give or receive expressions of love and affection?

   Very weak   Weak   Moderate   Strong   Very strong

   b. Who does The Kid prefer to initiate expressions of love and affection?

   Usually prefers for   Either way is   Usually prefers to
   others to approach   equally OK.   do the approaching

Now consider the answers you provided above, regarding the needs and preferences of your inner child in the areas of *inclusion, control,* and *affection.* Think about how you may need to adjust your style of relating in order to accommodate those needs and preferences. Express your thoughts and ideas in that regard by completing the sentences below.

Regarding *inclusion*:

I will remember that the child needs/wants …

_____

_____

_____

_____

I will remember that the child will not respond well to …

_____

_____

_____

_____

Regarding _control_:

I will remember that the child needs/wants ...

_____

_____

_____

_____

I will remember that the child will not respond well to ...

_____

_____

_____

_____

Regarding _affection_:

I will remember that the child needs/wants ...

_____

_____

_____

_____

I will remember that the child will not respond well to ...

_____

_____

_____

_____

Application

Question 7: How can I improve my relationship skills and apply them to my process of reparenting?

At the beginning of this chapter (in the eighth paragraph, to be specific), I mentioned four key factors that were considered in a certain lady's therapy. I said that when those four elements were corrected and became healthy, so did her relationships. Look back, and see what those four key factors were. List them below. (I have given you the initial for each factor to make it easier. You're welcome.)

1. I_____   3. T_____

2. S_____   4. P_____

Next, I mentioned that from these four factors, seven questions emerged. I listed the seven questions relevant to this chapter, and you have already processed six of them. As we consider the seventh and final question, we will draw from what you have learned and gained from this chapter so far.

From Question 1, you explored your primary identity and your best answer to the question, "Who am I?" according to your belief system at the time.

From Question 2, you explored your true identity as a child of God and made some progress toward accepting and realizing it.

From Question 3, you considered the tremendous importance of self-image, and you learned the three factors that determine it.

From Question 4, you learned three profound principles that can be applied in order to improve your self-image or that of your inner child.

From Question 5, you clarified the difference between temperament and personality and arrived at a working definition for our purposes.

From Question 6, you increased you relationship potential by expanding your knowledge of your inner child's needs and preferences in the areas of inclusion, control, and affection.

As you near the conclusion of this chapter, please read the following observations, and then initial each one that you will accept as truth and attempt to apply in your process of reparenting:

1. I understand that the process of reparenting depends largely upon a healthy working relationship between me (the adult) and the part of me we call the inner child. _____

2. I also understand that the more I know about my inner child, the better equipped I will be to relate to him or her. _____

3. I also understand that there are ways in which my inner child can and will change as he or she becomes less childish and more childlike. _____

4. I accept as truth the fact that such positive change depends greatly on my relationship skills and my willingness to lovingly apply them in my reparenting process. _____

5. I also accept as truth the fact that both my adult self and my inner child probably changed in some ways and for the better as we went through and processed the contents of this chapter. _____

6. I will try to be mindful of the factors that determine self-image and will attempt to strengthen and overcome the deficits I detect in my inner child by applying the three profound principles presented in this chapter. _____

7. As I continue my reparenting process, I will take into consideration what I have learned about the temperament and personality of my inner child. _____

8. As I complete the remaining chapters of this workbook, I will attempt to be lovingly aware of my inner child's needs and preferences in the areas of inclusion, control, and affection. _____

Finally, please read the following definitions of a loving relationship. They were written by clients of Dr. Leo Buscaglia and were published in *Redbook* several years ago. I have kept a copy because some of the expressions are so impressive and insightful. Most of them were written with a sweetheart or a marriage partner in mind. There are likely a few phrases or expressions, however, that could apply to the ideal relationship between an adult and his or her precious, little child within.

As you read the following statements, your assignment is to select a few phrases, ideas, or expressions that might characterize the relationship you would ultimately like to have with your inner child when your reparenting is complete. As you notice certain phrases or sentences that are impressive or seem to have possibilities for expressing your ideal relationship with your inner child, please underline them. You will be asked to use some of them in your final exercise of this chapter.

Defining a Loving Relationship

- A loving relationship is a choice partnership in which even imperfection is seen as possibility and therefore a thing of beauty; where discovery, struggle, and acceptance are the basis of continued growth and wonderment.

- A loving relationship is one in which you can be open and honest with another without fear of being judged. It's being secure in the knowledge that you are each other's best friend, and that no matter what happens, you will stand by each other.

- A loving relationship is one in which possessiveness gives way to allowing the other to be his/her own person; in which selfishness gives way to selfless giving, sharing, and caring; in which the lines of communication are always kept open; in which the good in each person is maximized, the bad minimized.

- A loving relationship is one in which each person allows a deep awareness of the other to grow between them, with the understanding that no one is perfect, but that love is perfect, and therefore, as the basic tool for relating, can solve all problems.

- A loving relationship is not defined by length of time, but rather by quality of caring. It is home for one's soul—a place to be ourselves and explore our deepest yearnings, hopes, fears, and joys without fear of rejection.

- A loving relationship is one in which the loved one is free to be himself, to laugh with me but never at me; to cry with me but never because of me; to love life, to love himself, to love being loved. Such a relationship is based upon freedom and can never grow in a jealous heart.

- A loving relationship is one in which you see the beloved not as an extension of self but as a unique forever-becoming beautiful individual—a situation in which the persons can bring their own special "I" to each other, a blending of selves without the fear of loss of self.

- A loving relationship is one that offers comfort in the silent presence of another with whom you share mutual trust, honesty, admiration, devotion, and that special thrill of happiness simply in being together.

Now, to conclude this chapter, look over the phrases, ideas, or sentences that you underlined above. Select a few of the ones that, in your opinion, best apply to the ideal relationship you would ultimately like to have with your inner child. Express this by writing a few sentences in the space below. Feel free to use your own words, if and when you wish.

Little Mona Did It

I didn't like Little Mona for a long time. We didn't have a bad relationship; we had *no* relationship at all! I couldn't tolerate her childishness. She was afraid of so many things, like life mostly! She even felt afraid of me. She was very fearful of abandonment, and she felt very angry at the non-protection and non-care that I gave her. This no-relationship wasn't working very well. The more that I ignored her, the louder her needs screamed out at me. She tried every childish way she knew to get my attention, but the more she acted out, the more I pushed her into the basement of my emotions.

Nobody at home was meeting her needs, so she eventually began looking elsewhere, to others, for those strokes of love and affection. She began to settle for any kind of attention she could get from anybody and pretended that it was love. I remember far too well the emotional (and sometimes physical) pain, disappointment, guilt, and confusion of those days of promiscuity. Maybe it was the shame we shared that finally brought us together, but Little Mona and I somehow agreed that some things had to change. So, together we decided to start looking for safer people.

That's how we found Dr. Gilliam. Then we looked around and found some other safe people, like Beth, Dr. Fontaine, Dr. Gotway, and Carrie. With time, Sue and Angela were added. Along with some others at Oak View Baptist Church, they provided me with some badly needed dental work. I began to realize that, through these people, God was loving both me and Little Mona. It was through Little Mona's childlike faith, though, that we were able to risk loving them back. That was scary! Especially the part about having a relationship with God. It took us awhile to learn and accept what grace really is about.

As I worked through this chapter, I began to understand who I was inside, and I began to accept my true identity. I felt afraid of some of the questions, but then I figured out why. It was because I still cared too much about what other people thought of me. The section on self-image helped me work through that. I noticed that the healthier my self-image became, the easier it became to accept Little Mona. I worked hard to develop the skills that allowed me to relate to her, even when she felt angry, threw fits, made mistakes, or acted out of fear rather than love. When I learned to accept her imperfections, I found that I could accept and appreciate all her wonderful and unique qualities as well.

In the final exercise of this chapter, here is the way I defined the loving relationship I desire to have with Little Mona: A loving relationship is a choice in which imperfection becomes a possibility for growth, and growth is beautiful. It is acceptance, not judgment; it allows a person to grow without controlling how they grow. Problems are temporary and able to be overcome. A loving relationship with myself allows me to be myself; to laugh with me, not at me; to cry with me, yet not be the cause of the tears; to love life, God, others, and self; to feel safe and secure enough to just relax and know that I am loved.

I am not just an extension of some other person, but am growing into my own person, and as a result, I have more to give. There is a peaceful comfort in the growing truth, honesty, admiration, devotion, and the joy of togetherness with God, others, and my precious, little, inner child.

Chapter 17

Completing the Adult's Part in Reparenting

Vantage Point

DORIS WAS A young mother in her late twenties. Her firstborn was a healthy little girl, who was four or five months old when Doris came for counseling. She explained that she was very concerned about her parenting and that she was afraid that she would do something wrong that would emotionally scar her daughter or leave some irreversible defect. She had read several books on the subject and had talked to several successful parents, but her fears remained, and her worry increased. Even advice and reassurance from her own mother did not seem to help.

It did help a little when her husband (the baby's father) became more involved and more supportive. It helped some more when, together, we developed a parenting strategy that they both could accept and embrace. But, interestingly enough, there was one particular insight that seemed to calm Doris's fears and provide her with focus and direction. *It was the simple realization that the single most important parenting thing she could do for her daughter was to provide her with a healthy mama!*

That idea somehow "scored" with Doris and launched her on a passionate mission to become the healthiest, happiest, and most well-adjusted mama possible. As a fringe benefit, she also became a healthy, happy, well-adjusted wife and human being in general!

As we prepare to complete your (the adult's) part in reparenting, I am urging you to accept the same challenge and perspective that made Doris an effective and successful parent ... and wife ... and human being! Please make this decision now, and make it official by reading, signing, and dating the following agreement:

"I realize that at this point, the single most important reparenting thing I can do for my inner child is to provide her or him with a healthy, well-adjusted, adult counter-part, and I hereby agree to apply myself seriously to that task."

_____   _____
          Signature of Adult   Date

Input from Dr. G.

Wow! Think about this: It is awesome to realize that this is the very first sentence you will read after officially agreeing to apply yourself seriously to the task at hand! This is also the first paragraph you will encounter after committing to become the best "reparent" you can possibly be for your little "child within." *This presents a perfectly precious point of pregnant potential to perceive and ponder some pertinent, profound principles that promote practical progress and personal proficiency in providing passionate, productive parenting practices with positive pay-offs toward completing the adult's part in the reparenting process.*

Now, please re-read the above, italicized, run-on sentence, and count the number of words in that sentence that start with the letter *p. (Your inner child will enjoy this. Keep reading, and I will tell you the answer shortly!)*

Next, re-read the long, italicized sentence, and try to pick out the main thing that sentence is actually saying. In two or three short, simple sentences, express below what you think the writer is trying to get across. *(This is an assignment for the adult. She or he will probably not enjoy it!)*

_____

_____

_____

_____

(Time out! Let The Kid write the number of "p words" she or he counted in the long sentence above: . The answer is ... twenty-five! If you counted correctly, write these words with your non-dominant hand: "Yea! I am smarter than a fifth-grader!")

Now, here is my short and simple version of the same long sentence above. (How does it compare with yours?) "Because you just made and signed a serious commitment, there is probably a readiness to act on it. That makes it a good time to learn something that will help you achieve your goal. You have a right, therefore, to expect something helpful, practical, and profound in the next few sentences!"

So, here is my attempt to meet that expectation. In other words, the next few paragraphs should give you a helpful, practical overview of this chapter, plus a little insight into the reasoning that causes us to limit its focus to one major subtopic.

If you remember the title of this chapter, write it here. (If you do not remember it, take a peek, and then write it here.)

This title, of course, reveals the primary purpose of this chapter. With this in mind, we established that the best way to accomplish this is to provide your inner child with the healthiest well-adjusted adult counter-part possible; so this becomes our primary goal. Next, because it is impossible to cover everything about anything, we will zero in on our primary objective, which will determine the primary focus of this chapter.

Of all the factors that could contribute to a healthy, well-adjusted adult counterpart, probably the most significant is the ability to make good, wise decisions. To foster, develop, and sharpen this skill, therefore, becomes our primary objective.

More specifically, the remainder of this chapter will be focusing on the subtopic of making healthy choices. For your practical consideration and application, you will be confronted with:

- The Potential of Healthy Choices.
- The Power of Healthy Choices.
- The Process of Healthy Choices.
- The Pay-off of Healthy Choices.

Other than my own Counseling and Seminar materials, my primary references are two workbooks by Christian psychiatrist Frank Minirth, M.D., Ph.D., founder and President of The Minirth Clinic, P.A., in Richardson, Texas. After you complete this volume of *Reparenting*, I would encourage you to consume both of these workbooks in their entirety:

Happiness Is A Choice Workbook and
The Power of Choices—The Normal Zone Workbook

Taking It Personally

The Potential of Healthy Choices

For many years I hosted a live, call-in, talk radio program. The name of that program was *Choices*. Each time we came on the air, a few seconds into the musical intro, I would open with the following statement: "You're tuned to a program called *Choices* … the live, call-in, talk radio program designed to help you make healthy choices … the kind that lead to the abundant life!"

There was more, but for now, let's focus on the words "the abundant life." I wrote a theme song for my seminar by that name, which included the following lyrics:

> I'm an over-comer, more than a survivor,
> Living the abundant life,
> I'm an over-comer, more than a survivor,
> Powered by the blood of Christ!
> Lots of people walking 'round but not really living,
> Lots of people talking love but not really giving,
> They have all their vital signs,
> But nothing in their life that shines,
> So, be an over-comer, more than a survivor,
> Living the abundant life!
> Living the abundant life!

It was Christ Himself who pointed out the difference between the abundant life and just living. Vital signs are good and necessary, but they are not enough. There is so much more abundantly available to you than just surviving, and whether you (and your inner child) experience it or not depends mainly on the choices you make.

I know of thirty verses of Scripture that reveal the many facets of the abundant life. I have included them in the appendix of this workbook.

Also, notice the potential suggested in the following statement made by Dr. Frank Minirth in his Workbook entitled, *Happiness Is A Choice:* "There are certain choices that a person can make that will lift a depressed mood. I've used seven of them through the last twenty-five years in my practice of Christian psychiatry. These seven choices which you may need to make or help someone else make, could change a life forever, moving you from depression to happiness. Actually, these choices apply not only to those who are depressed, but to all who are in pursuit of true happiness."

Consider also Dr. Minirth's remarks from his introduction to the workbook, *The Power of Choices—The Normal Zone Workbook:* "A normal zone does exist, and happiness depends on choosing to live in the normal zone … Legions of times I have seen people choose to stop addictions, focus better, eat more appropriately, become less manic, become less depressed, decrease paranoia, and act more appropriately. Sometimes choice can reign over both stress factors and even the genome. Of course, you who know me know that I don't just mean human will power; I mean choice enabled by God."

Yes, the potential is tremendous, and the dividends are high, while the other alternatives may be unhealthy, unwise, and often painful. That is probably why the following Scripture urges us to choose life! *"I call heaven and earth this day to record against you, that I have set before you life and death, blessing and cursing: therefore, choose life, that both thou and thy seed may live …" (Deuteronomy 30:19 mine).*

The Power of Healthy Choices.

It is again appropriate to refer to Dr. Minirth's workbook entitled, *The Power of Choices.* Following are the seven powerful choices he recommends for attaining and maintaining your health:

1. *Work on making healthy choices.* Some people live much longer than others because of healthy choices. Seniors over 100 years old attribute their longevity to being thin, not smoking or drinking, coping well with stress, having confidence, being independent, and having increased life satisfaction. People from oriental countries tend to live longer because of choices concerning diet, such as eating more fish (omega-3 fatty acids).
2. *Decrease stress.* Stress moves people out of the normal zone both physically and mentally. With stress inflammatory cytokines and autoantibodies increasing one is more likely to develop an autoimmune disease. Stress also lowers a chemical called *brain-derived neurotropic factor*, which nourishes the brain cells. Making decisions that decrease stress preserves memory, increases mood, reduces obesity, and improves physical health.
3. *Lose weight.* Two thirds of the population is overweight, and *one-third is obese.* Fat is a source of cytokines, which in adipose tissue can cause inflammation in other body tissues, such as in the heart. Losing weight can decrease other diseases and increase longevity and quality of life. Your first step is a choice.
4. *Exercise.* Exercise alters cytokines, reduces inflammatory effect, and helps both your heart and your mood.
5. *Improve cognition.* The mind and memory run everything. To stay in the normal zone, keep the mind and memory sharp through salubrious choices, i.e., those that are favorable to health or well-being.
6. *Ask God to keep you in the normal zone.* The stakes are high. You can do all these things through strength that Christ offers (Phil. 4:13).
7. *Continue making the good and healthy choices that are working for you.* List a few of the good and healthy choices that you have made, that you are making, or that you plan to make soon.

In conclusion, the following true story will demonstrate the awesome power of making good, healthy choices.

GHC #1: Caleb's parents called Dr. Minirth. They wanted help. Caleb had suffered from paranoid schizophrenia for several years. He did not look or act normal. Doctors had tried hard to help, but Caleb was going downhill. He had been placed in the back insanity unit, under high security and was receiving the strongest antipsychotics known to man.

GHC #2: The parents arranged to bring Caleb to the Minirth Clinic. He had flaccid (lacking energy) psychosis. His eyes rolled back in his head as he grunted at Dr. Minirth. His face was contorted, he was confused, and he had a cold stare.

GHC #3: Dr. Minirth cried out to God, saying, "God, I know biochemistry, but this is beyond me. Please help me help Caleb. Return him to the normal zone!"

GHC #4: Dr. Minirth went to work. He stopped a depot neuroleptic Caleb was on and started a new oral neuroleptic with possible cognitive enhancing effects. He also slowly stopped other medications that might be hurting Caleb's cognition—depakote, lithium, and valium were discontinued.

GHC #5: Caleb was placed in a ranch setting, where others would teach him social skills. His dad assisted as Caleb learned to smile, engage others socially, and take better care of himself.

GHC #6: Caleb was re-assessed after four months and was found to be 80 percent back to the normal zone.

GHC #7: Caleb and his family continued to follow medical advice and to practice good mental health care, demonstrating once again the awesome power of making good, healthy choices.

—Copied and abbreviated from Minirth workbook, *The Power of Choices.*

Application

The Process of Healthy Choices

Notice above that this section is called *Application*. This section of each chapter takes on the flavor of a laboratory experience. It involves something (or some things) to go and do and apply. It includes action-type answers to the question "So what?"

Now, look again, find the word *Process*, and circle it. (It's right under the word *Application*. You're welcome.) This implies an action-type answer to the question "How?"

You may want to take a break and come back fresh, because we are about to mix the "So what" with the "How" and stir briskly!

Transitional Point: *There is a great difference between knowing how to do something and actually getting yourself to do it. In Scripture, James wrote about people who know how to do good but do not do it. His conclusion was, "To him it is sin," i.e., a sin of omission (James 4:17). The solution is to make good decisions, and your will is the key! Prepare to learn the process and to apply it.*

There is a story about three frogs that sat on a lily pad. One of them decided to jump off, into the water. How many were left? Write the logical answer here: ___. The correct answer is three. The story goes that there were still three frogs left because the one that decided to jump off never got around to actually doing it.

The argument could be made that he did not actually decide to do it if it never happened. That may be true, but *he intended to do it!* He just never exercised his will and made the choice to jump! I repeat: *your will is the key!*

"To will or not to will, that is the question!" Your will, of course, is the part of you that makes decisions. Think of it as your "steering will." (Pun intended.) It is not your mind, so it doesn't come up with ideas of its own. It's not your emotions, so it doesn't have strong feelings about things. It considers the thoughts and logic that come from your mind. It also considers the feelings that your emotions may be expressing (or screaming) at the moment. Then, normally, your will makes a decision. When your mind and your emotions want the same thing, the decision is easy. When they disagree, the will usually chooses one of these three options:

1. It may choose to do what your mind is wanting to do.
2. It may choose to do what your emotions are wanting to do.
3. It may choose to do nothing at all.

If you choose to do nothing at all, then the issue is remanded back to the mind and emotions for further conversation or argumentation. This interaction is called "self-talk," and it can become rather heated. It is usually internal dialog, but it can be processed externally, in which case a person may talk aloud to herself/himself or may bring other people into the conversation. I have heard people have entire arguments all by themselves. Ordinarily, they will eventually come to some conclusion, make a decision, and then put it into action as behavior.

So, why is it so hard to make good choices, and why do so many people fail at this? I'm glad you asked! Those are the right questions, and they deserve a clear and concise answer. *I believe that the major problem is a situation based on a false belief.* Let me explain.

The *situation* is that most people are far too strongly committed to their feelings and emotions. If humanly possible, most people will not act in violation to their feelings and emotions. They do this naturally and automatically because their feelings represents what they want; and most human beings are generally dedicated to doing what they want and getting what they want, when they/we can. In fact, the most frequent reason for experiencing anger is because people do not get what they want, not necessarily what they need. This human characteristic cannot be overemphasized, as it is ingrained in the warp and woof of human nature. The sad fact is that most people are feelings worshippers.

The basic *false belief* behind this situation is the belief that how I feel is who I am. If I am counseling someone who continues to say, "I am depressed," I will eventually object and require that person to say, "I feel depressed." I may say to them, "Depression is not who you are, it is how you feel." Depression is not his/her true identity, and I must not let him/her get by with the false belief that how he/she feels is who he/she is. If so, that person's identity will shift each time his/her emotions change, and that person will likely remain unstable.

To make matters even worse, this basic false belief spawns other offspring that gang up and work against good decision-making. Related false beliefs emerge, and a network of error may expand and unfold as follows:

1. If how I feel is who I am, then I need to be dedicated, true, and honest to my feelings.
2. If I do not remain dedicated, true, and honest to my feelings, I am at least dishonest and am probably a fraud and a hypocrite.
3. If I choose to behave in ways that don't match my feelings, I am being a fake, and that is as wrong as being a fraud and a hypocrite.
4. Even if I choose to do something that is good and right, if it doesn't match my feelings, then my heart is not in it, so it's either deceptive or it doesn't count, so I should not do it.
5. If I go against the way I feel, I have violated who I really am and have betrayed my true self; therefore, I don't deserve to be happy, and I should feel guilty and ashamed.
6. If I *feel* guilty, then I *am* guilty, and I deserve to be punished. And if no one else punishes me, then I should somehow punish myself.

Obviously, not everyone holds all of these false beliefs, but many of my clients have had all of these, plus others, in their belief systems.

Please underline this in your book and in your mind: *When an idea is in your belief system, regardless of whether it is true or false, accurate or inaccurate, it is the reality to you, and it is the reality to which everything inside you responds.* (Chew that up, and swallow it.)

NOTE: Examine the false beliefs above. If you recognize any of them as your own, write them below. If you think of any others that may be hindering your decision-making, list them also. It is recommended that you contact a counselor to work with you on correcting these false beliefs. People are rarely successful in altering their own belief systems alone.

_____

_____

_____

_____

The final complication of our dilemma is as follows: *Your will is a part of you, so it ultimately trusts your belief system. When your belief system is polluted or infected with the errors we have discussed, your emotions, your desires, and your will get welded or fused together in such a way that what you want feels like what you need. Your will interprets that as what you must have, and tends to obediently and unquestionably choose the option of doing what your emotions are wanting to do.*

(Ponder ... process ... and proceed!)

Look back over the last seven or eight paragraphs. Then use the space below to express briefly, in your own words, why it is so hard to make good choices and why so many people fail at it. (Your opinion matters.)

_____

_____

_____

_____

Now that we understand the challenge, let us get prepared to meet it.

Earlier I stated emphatically that your will is the key. That statement assumes that you understand that God gave you a will and the power to use it to make choices. Joshua instructed God's people to make a choice (Josh. 24:15). Paul observed that putting a choice into action requires a willing mind, but added that there must first be a readiness to will (2 Cor. 8:11–12). So, get ready to exercise your will!

Think of your will as if it were a muscle.
Like a muscle, your will needs to be exercised to be strong and usable.
You must learn to "wiggle your will" in order to exercise it.
Compare it to a guy who has learned to wiggle his nose or his ears.
(I would demonstrate this skill for you, if I were there!)
Now compare it to a skillful typist, instrumentalist, or martial artist.
Their finesse and control were gained through practice and exercise.
Your ability to "wiggle and control your will" is necessary
in order to make good choices, especially the hard ones!
(So, put a tennis shoe on your head so you can jog your mind!)
Ready ... set ... EXERCISE!

Will Exercise Assignment

What is it?

Answer: A week-long commitment to do (or not do) and/or say (or not say)
three specific things that you will choose.

Conditions:
1. These three things must be clearly defined.
2. The commitment must require a little will power.
3. It must not require too much will power! You *must* succeed!
4. It must be worded in a way that enhances the probability of success.
    (For example, instead of promising to write one thank you note each day, you could
    promise to write seven notes during the next seven days.)
5. It is best not to choose something that fights a basic drive, an addiction,
    or a well-established habit. Remember, the purpose
    of this assignment is to locate your will and "wiggle that muscle"
    successfully for seven days!

Here are a few examples of things people have chosen in the past: To drink a certain amount
of water daily, not to drink more than one carbonated beverage per day (or seven per week), to
walk or do some exercise, to do a good deed, to read a prescribed number of Scripture verses,
not to eat carbs, to make up a bed, to tell someone you love him/her, to sort or clean something,
to complete a project, to keep a certain routine, or hundreds of other things that would make
someone feel glad or better or successful.

Worksheet

Date project to begin: _____ Date project will end: _____

Commitment No. 1

Thoughts and ideas: _____

_____

Final wording: _____

_____

Commitment No. 2

Thoughts and ideas: _____

_____

Final wording: _____

_____

Commitment No. 3

Thoughts and ideas: _____

_____

Final wording: _____

_____

Use this space to write notes to yourself about strategy, preparation, things you may need, things to remember, reminders, etc.:

_____

_____

_____

_____

Summary Report After Assignment is Completed

How did it go? What was hardest about it? Anything surprise you? Anything go wrong? Anything happen that was funny, sad, or embarrassing? What is something you learned about yourself? Were you successful? Anything you would do differently if you were doing it again?

What feelings did you experience, and why? Did you have to require yourself to behave in opposition to your feelings? How did you get yourself to do it? Do you think you understand what your will is? Can you "wiggle" it? Is there anything else that you need to report?

_____

_____

_____

_____

Most people need to do this assignment two more times, changing at least one commitment each time so that you are slightly increasing the total amount of will power required. The same conditions apply, and the same summary report should be written each time after the assignment is completed. *If you did not succeed in your first attempt, you should definitely require yourself to experience the second and third attempts. This is a necessary component in completing chapter 17.*

NOTE: Forms for assignments two and three are not included in this workbook. Feel free to make copies of these worksheets, or simply use your own paper and staple it to your workbook when you are done.

If you participated in the Will Exercises seriously and as requested, you likely encountered a part of yourself that seems to have a mind of its own. That part of you wants what it wants when it wants it. It often opposes and resists what you know to be the best choices, and it usually somehow gets the support and endorsement of your feelings.

The apostle Paul was very familiar with this part of himself, and he described it well in the last few verses of Romans, chapter seven. He said that even when he wanted to do right, there was something deep within him, in his lower nature, that was at war with his mind and often won the battle (verse 23). I have been told that St. Francis of Assisi called this resistant, stubborn, donkey-like part of himself "Brother Ass."

For the purposes of this workbook, I am going to call that part of you, your *wanter*. Somebody said, "If you give it an inch, it will become your ruler!" If you let it reign, you will pursue and do many bad things. Those bad things are listed in Galatians 6:17–21. Your wanter is very self-centered, self-focused, self-serving, and generally selfish. All it can do is want; but no matter what or how much you give it, it can never be satisfied or fulfilled for long. It will always want more. That's why I call it your wanter.

In regard to the part of you that operates your will, I am going to call that your *willer*. It is the part of you that sets your decisions into motion and allows them to become realities. It releases the energy that puts your choices into action and causes them to become actual behaviors.

So, if and when your *wanter* and your *willer* get together and team up, they become an irresistible force. In other words, when they "gang up and get going," humanly speaking, there is nothing inside you that can stop them. Good or bad, right or wrong, *something going to happen!* (Wow and double wow!)

Transitional Point: *Do you get it that your wanter and your willer cannot be trusted together as a couple? They do not usually bring out the best in each other. A courtship between them would likely wreak much havoc, and their marriage could hardly be one made in heaven!*

Warning! This is a high drop-out danger point! A lot of people bog down and stop working along about here! The inner child does not understand what we are talking about, the inner adolescent has lost interest, and adults are not too excited about interfering in the relationship between their own wanters and willers. In essence, they don't want to deprive their wanter of what their wanter wants, and they won't! (Can you say that last sentence three times without laughing?)

Since this part of the chapter is of massive importance to understanding the process of making healthy choices, I have chosen the universal languages of music and humor to re-engage the reader. The familiar, lighthearted melody should entertain your inner child. The unique set of humorous lyrics should trip the fancy of your inner adolescent. And it is hoped that you, the adult, will consider and appreciate the slightly hidden truths that are encoded in and between the lines of the song.

"Song of the Wanter and the Willer"
By Dr. Larry Gilliam

(This song is to be sung to the melody of "Do-Re-Mi," as sung
by Maria and the children in the movie, *Sound of Music*.)

When your wanter and your willer
Get together, it's a killer!
When you ask, "What do I want?"
That's a great big honkin' DON'T!
Cause it activates your will,
Which anticipates a thrill,
Starts it rolling down a hill,
And it sets in motion ... STUFF!

And the stuff it sets in motion,
Makes like waves upon your ocean!
On your ocean of emotion,
Setting off a large commotion;
And you do some things you shouldn't,
And some things you usually wouldn't,
And a few things that you couldn't ...
If you had not started ... STUFF!

And it started down the hill
Cause your wanter hugged your will,
(and) set in motion lots of stuff,
(Of) which they'll never get enough,
(Cause) all that they can do is want,
(And) they've forgotten how to DON'T!
And they can never be fulfilled,
(They'll always) seek another thrill,

Nothing will ever satisfy, And that is why they have to DIE!

(Note: A recording of this song and a few other songs that reflect the therapeutic humor of Dr. Larry Gilliam are available through the Dayspring Counseling Service in Irving, Texas.)

1. Look carefully at the wording of verse number one.
   What is one of the lines that is most impressive to you, and why?

   _____

   _____

   _____

   _____

   What seems to be the main thing this verse is trying to say?

   _____

   _____

   _____

   _____

2. Look carefully at the wording of verse number two.
   What is one of the lines that is most impressive to you, and why?

   _____

   _____

   _____

   What seems to be the main thing this verse is trying to say?

   _____

   _____

_____

_____

3. Look carefully at the wording of verse number three.
    What is one of the lines that is most impressive to you, and why?

    _____

    _____

    _____

    _____

    What seems to be the main thing this verse is trying to say?

    _____

    _____

    _____

    _____

4. Look carefully at the wording of the couplet that concludes the poem.
    At first glance, what do these two lines seem to mean?

    _____

    _____

    _____

    _____

    Can you tell that they are a metaphor and not meant to be taken literally?

    Circle one: Yes No Maybe Other: _____

What are some questions that are raised or left unanswered by these two final lines?

_____

_____

_____

_____

Next, let me compliment you on figuring out the questions! Asking the right questions is a major part of getting the right answers. It is likely that the questions you listed will be answered in the remainder of this chapter; if not, we would welcome your contact at the Dayspring Counseling Office in Irving, Texas. You probably included questions much like the one that follows, but I would like to word it like this for our consideration here:

"So, why does the last line of the song say, "And that is why they have to die?"
There is a *pretty good answer* and a *really good answer* to this question. There is a way, however, in which both answers require something or someone to die.

The *pretty good answer* is practical, down-to-earth, and can be a handy, temporary fix at times. It requires you to use your will to die to a personal desire or emotion. It is necessary when life's circumstances present you with options that require you to choose against what you prefer, what you want, and sometimes what you need. Like in the Will Exercises, you find your will, and you use it to make a choice that is contrary to your feelings and sometimes self-sacrificial. You have your reasons for doing this, and then you use your will once again to deal with the feelings that result, or you numb out in order to cope or you turn it over to the Lord or all of the above. This is the *pretty good answer* as to why your wanter and your willer have to die, and this approach to dying will often keep you functional through some difficult times and some hard decisions.

Apply this approach to people having to Deal with the following life circumstances. How do they feel, what choices might they make, and how might they use their wills in order to cope? In what ways might they have to die to certain personal desires or emotions? Think through these scenarios, and then discuss at least three of them with a person of your choice:

- Someone who loves sweets finds out that he/she is diabetic.
- A girl has to choose between two men, both of whom she is very fond.
- A mother's only child has just moved away to go to college.
- Someone's doctor just told him that he must lose at least twenty pounds.
- A thirteen-year-old is having to decide which divorced parent to live with.

- An employee's boss is often verbally abusive, but she really needs the job.
- A person in her fifties is having to take care of her aging mother.
- A person with a strong habit or addiction is trying to quit.
- A person sacrifices fame and fortune to accept God's call to ministry.
- Other: _____

Initial here to show that you have completed this assignment: _____

There is also *a really good answer*, and I need to be sure you are ready for it. We have boldly and repeatedly proclaimed that when your wanter and your willer join forces to pursue a goal, and they reach a certain momentum, there is nothing in your humanness that is powerful enough to stop them. They will nearly always have their way. The answer is not for you to run faster, try harder, or grunt louder. It is to tap into a power source much greater than your own, one that is available to every born-again believer. At the same time, this same transaction will pull the plug on your wanter and your willer! It will kill their engines and disconnect them from their power supplies, so to speak. This is the *really good answer*! It is a better answer because (1) it is God's answer, (2) it works each time you meet the conditions, and (3) the payoff is so much better!

The Pay-off of Healthy Choices

With this in mind, let's talk about the pay-off and the conditions for receiving it (not necessarily in that order). More specifically, let's allow the remainder of this chapter to unfold in the following order and sequence:

1. Who and what has to die?
2. Who and what gets to come alive as a result?
3. How and why it can happen
4. The profoundly positive pay-off of the process

> **Transitional Point:** *We are now approaching our destination, and there is not a lot of runway. There is little or no margin for error. We anticipate a smooth, safe landing. We must keep in mind, however, that our other option is to crash and burn. Seriously.*

1. Who and what has to die?
   In the last line of the song, when it says, "They have to die," it is talking about the alliance that connects your will and the emotional part of your soul (where your wanter is located), which empowers them to control, abuse, and terrorize the rest of your being. This combo is what the apostle Paul called "the flesh," and arrangements have already been made for its execution (Galatians 2:20 and 5:24).

Scripture has a lot to say about something or someone having to die so that something or someone else can come alive. Compare this to some people who are being held captive by some terrorists. They are in bondage, totally controlled, and are often abused and terrorized by their captors. Suppose that a team of Navy Seals comes and kills the terrorists; releases the captives; gives them food, medicine, and other necessities; and eventually returns them to their homes and their loved ones. I don't think those people would have a hard time with the theology that something or someone may have to die so that something or someone else can live again.

You tend to feel alive and well when your mind and spirit are set free.

2. Who and what gets to come alive as a result?
Scripture talks specifically about dying to self, the flesh, and certain impulses. *The point is that life and death are mutually exclusive, so we have to die to the things of death in order to come alive to the things of life!* (Romans 6 and 7 are filled with these kinds of dichotomies, i.e., dying to something in order to come alive to something else.) *In this regard, the right choices will release power and life into our systems. This is a heap big pay-off!* Our task is to get this condition from theological truth into experiential reality. It can be done!

This kind of *"dying in order to live"* is possible because of what Christ has already done for us on the cross: "I am crucified with Christ, nevertheless I live; yet not I but Christ liveth in me …" (Gal. 2:20). This means that "our flesh was crucified with Him, along with all its affections and lusts" (Gal. 5:24). It also means that there is a power source infusing life into our beings, namely, from His Spirit into ours! Even if you do not understand this, it is available to you as a believer (Rom. 8:10–16).

Sometimes I compare the flesh to the Frankenstein monster: You can't kill him because he is already dead. He's dead, but he still behaves. He has to be "managed" and "given no occasion to act out," until he is ultimately eliminated.

Meanwhile (and some whiles are meaner than others), we must repeatedly meet the conditions that release divine power and life into our systems. The apostle Paul said, "I die daily …" (1 Cor. 15:31). Jesus Himself said to deny self and take up your cross each day (Luke 9:23). This must become a way of life for the victorious Christian.

3. How and why can this happen?
Now we need to talk in everyday language about the conditions that allow these things to become a reality in our lives. Exactly what is meant by words like *I die daily, deny yourself,* and *take up your cross each day?* Why do words like *yield, submit, surrender,* and *turn loose* keep showing up in the conversation? As one man pointed out, "None of those words sound very appealing or victorious to me!" That would be true, but neither do

labor pains seem worthwhile until that new bundle of life has arrived and been received into the arms and heart of its mother.

I would not presume that I could improve upon the words of Jesus when He said, "Except a corn of wheat fall to the ground and die, it abides alone: but if it die, it brings forth much fruit" (John 12:24). Some of that fruit is listed in Galatians five, and the first three on the list are genuine love, a deep-seated joy, and a peace that exceeds human understanding. Who would not sacrifice one grain of wheat to receive an entire sheaf in its place?

Or who would hesitate to bury one kernel of corn in order to grow an entire stalk with many ears of corn? I will tell you who would not: It would be the man or woman who has no faith that it would grow. It would be the one who does not understand that it would be an investment with many returns. In fact, when you are dealing with people, it becomes an investment that will draw interest for eternity!

Finally, let's re-emphasize the fact that one of the conditions is to make a major decision. It is a decision similar to the one that Moses presented to the children of Israel in Deuteronomy 30:19, when he said to them:

"I have set before you life and death, blessing and cursing: therefore, choose life, that both you and your descendants may live …"

The nitty-gritty of making such a choice is implied in Luke 20:17–18, where Jesus is represented as the chief cornerstone. In that parable, there are two choices in relation to that stone. One is to fall voluntarily on that stone and be broken. The other is for that stone to fall on us and grind us to powder. Neither of those options sounds very appealing, *unless* you understand three things as they relate to our application:

1. It is not talking about a part of your body that gets broken or crushed; it is talking about your self-will.
2. The first option represents a voluntary yielding or submitting of your will to His. If you refuse this option, however, you will likely be choosing the other option; namely, the drawn out, maybe lifelong process of "grinding."
3. In either case, the motive is to unleash the life, power, blessings, and fruit of the Spirit in your life … soon! *It will be so worth it, in this life and in the next!*

Through the years, many hymns and Christian songs have been written about choosing to yield, submit, surrender, or otherwise commit one's will, life, and fortune to God. A few that come to my mind immediately are " I Surrender All," "Not My Will," "Have Thine Own Way," and "No Turning Back." You can find many more in a song book, on the internet, or by asking your worship leader. *Please do this;* take a look at the lyrics, and listen to a few of them, if possible. Use the space below to list the names of three or four of the songs that were impressive to you.

_____

_____

_____

_____

4. What is the profoundly positive pay-off of the process?
    There are several.

    First, there is your personal achievement of the purpose of the chapter, as revealed in the chapter title: Completing the Adult's Part in the Process of Reparenting. This in itself is a noteworthy accomplishment, and your inner child will benefit directly through greater healing and wholeness.

    Second, there is your attainment of the primary objective to provide your inner child with the healthiest well-adjusted adult counterpart possible, which focuses on developing and sharpening your skills in making good, wise decisions. This process pays dividends as you experience the potential and the power of making healthy choices.

    Next, allow me to quote myself briefly, from a few pages back, on the subject of dying to one thing in order to come alive to something much better: *"In this regard, the right choices will release power and life into our systems. This is a heap big pay-off!"* (Amen.) This can mean freedom from the control of the "wanter-willer alliance," daily awareness of the nine "fruit of the Spirit," and the other blessings and benefits of "the abundant life"!

    Finally, there is the on-going, ultimate pay-off of greater intimacy with God. However good that may sound to you, it is even better! The Psalmist says it like this: "You will show me the path of life: in Your presence is the fullness of joy; at Your right hand there are pleasures forevermore!" (Ps. 16:11). ('Nuff said. What would you do for an encore?)

    This may be a good time and place for a prayer. Why not take a few moments now for that purpose, and then use the space below to summarize what you said, asked for, or committed to? You may need to look back later and remember. (You can think of it as your pray-off for the pay-off.)

_____

_____

_____

_____

Let's conclude this chapter with a comparison and contrast.

Transitional Point: *Through much of this chapter, I have referred to the alliance that fuses together your* wanter *and your* willer *and gives them the power to bully and control the rest of your being. It is like the tail being able to wag the dog. You will remember (I hope) that a few pages back, I mentioned that this alliance may be compared to "the flesh" as that term is used by Paul in Romans (chapters 6 and 7) and Galatians (chapter 5). This understanding will allow you to appreciate the comparison and contrast revealed in the songs that follow.*

The lifestyle resulting from the influence of "the flesh" follows:

Song of the Flesh
(To the tune of "Dark As A Dungeon")

Oh, listen to me, and I'll show you a life
Of unbridled passion, pleasure and strife,
Of self-satisfaction, indulgence and greed,
Complete disregard for the law or a creed.
I have no concern for what others may do
'Cause I'm tucked away safely, a-way down in you!

So, forget about others and listen to me,
Just do what you want and take what you see.
I state my position without fear or dread,
For I'm tucked away safely, way down in your head!

For I am your "flesh," a real part of you!
Just give me control and see what I do—
For I care not for law, religion, or morals,
I'm not scared of gossip or juries or quarrels.
Just do what you want with whatever you find,
For I'm tucked away safely, way down in your mind.

So, forget about others and listen to me,
Just do what you want and take what you see.
I state my position without fear or dread,
For I'm tucked away safely, a-way down in your head!

Yes, forget about morals and take my advice …
Just do what you feel, and then pay the price!

Your Summary Statement: In your own words, write two or three sentences to summarize the "Song of the Flesh." In other words, answer this question: What would a person's life be like if it were lived under the influence and control of "the flesh"?

_____

_____

_____

_____

For contrast and comparison, let's look at "The Flesh Versus the Spirit"
The lifestyle resulting from the influence of "the spirit" follows:

Song of the Spirit
(To the tune of "Dark As A Dungeon")

NOTE: This song was composed to fit the exact same tune and meter as "The Song of the Flesh" to emphasize the "either/or," optional aspect of flesh control versus Spirit control over a person's life.

Oh, listen to me, and I'll show you the way
To find rest and peace at the end of the day,
To know what real love is, with a conscience that's clear,
And a deep-seated joy that shines through each tear.
And all through the journey, I'll be there to guide you,
Cause I'm tucked away safely, a-way down inside you!

So, forget about fairness, and listen to me,
Forgive and show mercy and soon you will see
Why I state my position without fear or dread,
Cause I'll heal all the pain in your heart and your head!

For I am your spirit, a real part of you,
Just give *me* control and see what *I* do!
I'll strengthen your faith and restore all your morals.
I'll calm your confusion and settle your quarrels.
I'll bring you deliverance. I'll loose, and I'll bind.
I'll unravel troublesome thoughts in your mind!

So, forget about vengeance and listen to me,
Just yield to God's Spirit, and soon you will see
A life filled with purpose and passion and power,
Relief and refreshing from that very hour,
Fulfilled and filled full with the fruit of the Spirit;
And every believer with ears, let them hear it!

You'll never regret that you took my advice,
Cause whatever it takes will be well worth the price!

Your Summary Statement: In your own words, write two or three sentences to summarize the "Song of the Spirit." In other words, answer this question: What would a person's life be like if it were lived under the influence and control of "the Spirit"?

_____

_____

_____

_____

Notice that earlier in the lyrics, I referred to "your spirit" and started the word with a lower case letter, as I just did in this sentence. Yet, toward the end, I referred to "God's Spirit" and started the word with a capital letter. That is proper and on purpose, and it represents a great point with which to conclude this chapter.

The reference from earlier in the song says this: "For I am your spirit, a real part of you, Just give me control and see what I do!"

In this song, the spirit of the person can do wonderful things because it is filled, controlled, and empowered by the Spirit of God, as described in the later reference, as follows: "Just yield to God's Spirit and soon you will see…"

The question we all face on a daily basis is this: To which force will we yield the control of our lives? It depends on the choices we make. "Choose you this day …" "Choose life …"

Little Mona Did It

I am not known for my great choices in life. Although I've made some good choices along the way, far too often I've substituted "My will be done" for "Thy will be done"! Little Mona's usual feelings do not usually lead to the best decisions.

Most of the time, she feels deprived, lonely, and scared. Other times, she just feels angry, especially when others make choices that affect her, but she has no say in them. Then when people try to tell her (rather than ask her) what she thinks or how she feels, resentment is added to the anger, and things are pretty well set for a bad decision and some acting out.

Add to this the exhaustion of going seven days a week for most of the month and three people wanting me to be three places at the same time, and you have the recipe for a ticking time bomb. The remaining question is whether it will show up as a series of small explosions (such as ripping up my phone card) or one large blast. (God help the next person who looks crossways at me!)

I realize that a lot of these feelings and strange behaviors are fear based, but just knowing that does not make them any easier to handle. Fear feeds on itself, gets stronger and stronger, and can grow until you will do nearly anything to get some relief.

Overwhelming fear has led me to some unhealthy choices with food and prescription drugs. People say that addictions and suicide are not options, but to me, both were options. They were not good choices, but they were still choices. Unfortunately, a person *can* choose to take a drink, get on drugs, or attempt suicide. Fortunately, and by the grace of God, I "failed" at all three of these!

I knew someone who was not so fortunate. She had talked about hearing voices telling her to jump out of this eleven-story window. She said, "You do not know what it is like to hear these voices telling you to jump." I admit that I don't know about that, but I know that she could have chosen not to jump, and I know that she could have chosen to go inpatient for help. I also know that the terrible choice that she made was irreversible. You can't decide later that it was bad and somehow go back and change it. Also, you can't go back and "unhurt" the people who love and care about you.

When I get in the victim mode, I think that I have no choices, and I feel powerless and out of control emotionally. When I focus on who I really am and how I can use my will, Little Mona and I feel stronger, empowered, and in control. This helps us make good and healthy choices.

In a way, this could be the most important chapter in the workbook, because we all will have to keep making decisions the rest of our lives! I will finish, therefore, with this reminder from Deuteronomy 30:19: "I have set before you life and death, blessing and cursing: therefore, choose life, that both you and your descendants may live."

Chapter 18

Planning and Allowing for the Role Other People Must Play in Completing the Process of Reparenting

Vantage Point

IT SEEMS WISE and appropriate to begin this chapter by calling your attention to a few sentences from the Introduction of this workbook. The following selected excerpts should focus your perspective and prepare your mental set "backstage" for the curtains to open on Chapter 18:

> Deep inside you, there is a part of you that still thinks, feels, and reacts like you did as a child. That emotional child, wounded or healthy, will stay with you throughout your whole life, and it is that part of you which is the most sensitive to the pain you experienced earlier in your life ...

> You see, time alone does not bring about healing to these kinds of wounds. There are actually steps and a process that you must go through to nurture and to heal the child within you ... It is possible ... even today, to tap into three effective resources for the reparenting roles of nurturance, affirmation, and guidance that allow the vulnerable, little inner child to grow and experience healing. One resource is your adult self, the second is another caring person or support group and the third is God Himself.

> When you accept your personal role in allowing this to happen, tap the resources of another caring person and apply the biblical principles, which allow God to fulfill the missing dimensions, your reparenting can be completed. You will then find that, in this regard, it is really "never too late to have a happy childhood!"

Please read, once again, the sentence that is underlined above. Notice next that the workbook to this point has centered on and around the role of the first resource, namely, your adult self. Now it is time to shift the spotlight to the role that other people must play in completing the process. The fact that only one chapter is dedicated to this purpose does not suggest that it is less important. It is definitely a necessary link in the chain, and who can say that any link is expendable? In fact, I have heard it said that any chain is only as strong as its weakest link!

I would rather you approach Chapter 18 with this attitude: "Because there is only one chapter on this subject, I must take it really seriously!" Thank you.

Input from Dr. G.

Back in 1991, the doctors of the Minirth-Meier Clinic pooled some of the proven interactive techniques they used in their clinic and published a book and workbook entitled *Love Is A Choice*. Those publications were designed to foster recovery from codependent relationships, and they included a chapter entitled "Reparenting." There are four or five pages in that chapter that influenced my thinking significantly in regard to the role of other people in completing the process of reparenting. I am hereby giving due acknowledgment that a few pages in this chapter, and especially the next few paragraphs, likely reflect some good ideas and approaches that I absorbed while reading or using that publication with clients.

The workbook pointed out, for example, that we all have certain people we look up to, that those people may not realize how important they are to us, but that we watch them, learn from them, and take special notice of the comments they make to us. It was further noted that these people are nurturing us, whether they (or we) are aware of it or not, and that there may be some good candidates for "reparents" among these people of influence in our lives.

Take a few moments and write the names or initials of four or five people who had special, positive influence on your life at some impressionable time or times in the past. (Note: they may or may not still be around.)

Write names or initials of those who influenced you. Still available? Comments:

_____

_____

_____

_____

Add the names of a several others who are presently available, who might be good candidates for your "other people":

_____

_____

_____

_____

Examine all the people you listed on both lists above. (1) Put a check mark by each one that is a good listener or sounding board. (2) Next, put a check mark by all that you can safely trust with a secret or something confidential. (3) Now, put a check mark by all who will probably give you unconditional, non-judgmental support. (4) Next, put a check mark by the ones who will nearly always make themselves available when you need them. (5) Then, put a check mark by the ones who will gently but firmly confront you when you need it. (6) Finally, you may add one more check mark by the names of one or two people who deserve it because of some other special quality they have to offer.

Notice how you distributed the check marks among the names. Analyze how and where they stacked up. Use the space below to list the people who still seem to be good candidates for the supportive role of "other people" to help you complete your reparenting.

_____

_____

_____

_____

Here are some additional tips from the *Love Is A Choice* workbook as you continue your process of selecting supportive "other people":

1. Be very cautious about choosing someone of the opposite sex. If there is the slightest hint of a romantic entanglement, it would be wise to remove that person from your list. When parental nurturance becomes confused with sexual fulfillment, the resulting pain and disappointment can be almost as devastating as incest.

2. It is wise to choose people who are relatively healthy emotionally and spiritually. It would be best not to choose anyone who is less healthy than you are!
3. It is usually best not to choose close family members. Often they are too close to be objective, or they may have emotional baggage similar to yours.
4. Keep in mind that all people are human and will fail you in some way. Even the ones you respect the most may let you down or fail to meet your expectations. If you depend too heavily on other people, you can set yourself up for hurt and disappointment. There is safety in having at least four or five different people in your support system.
5. It is good to identify some support groups or organizations in your area. A church fellowship is a must, but also check out some other reputable groups, and give one or two of them an opportunity to be helpful. During the process, you might just find yourself being a blessing to someone else too!

List some reputable groups or organizations in your area that seem to have potential for offering appropriate support for you as you complete your reparenting. If you need help, try the internet, try yellow pages, or simply ask some people who might know. *After you list a few, circle two or three that you would be willing to check out personally.*

_____

_____

_____

_____

Initial here after you have followed through and actually checked out at least two of the groups or organizations listed above: Date:

Taking It Personally

Now you are probably set for the *Final Screening* to determine who your "other people" should be.

Actually, it might be more accurate to say that this *Final Screening* should determine who your "other people" should *not* be! That would likely be more accurate because we are going to identify and remove from consideration any *unsafe people* who may still be on your list.

Dr. Henry Cloud and Dr. John Townsend have authored a book and a workbook entitled *Safe People* (published by Zondervan). In this publication, they listed twenty traits of *unsafe people*.

Based on their list, I have gleaned and slightly tweaked the following fourteen characteristics, which seem most likely to work against a person's effectiveness as a "reparent":

1. Unsafe people think they "have it all together" and seem to have a hard time admitting their own faults or weaknesses.
2. Unsafe people may be religious but are not necessarily spiritual.
3. Unsafe people often get defensive rather than being open to feedback.
4. Unsafe people may come across as self-righteous rather than humble.
5. Unsafe people may apologize but not change their behavior.
6. Unsafe people tend to demand trust instead of earning it.
7. Unsafe people may build a dependence upon themselves, rather than encouraging freedom and independence in others.
8. Unsafe people may use flattering words but seem to lack empathy or genuine concern for others.
9. Unsafe people may tend to stay in parent/child roles, rather than growing and maturing in their relationships.
10. Unsafe people may have a hard time keeping secrets or maintaining confidentiality; instead, they may tend to gossip or "talk too much."
11. Unsafe people seem to have more of a negative or critical attitude, rather than a positive or encouraging influence.
12. Unsafe people may reveal impatience, intolerance, or anger, rather than showing healthy emotional boundaries.
13. Unsafe people may disclose too much too soon about themselves, instead of showing healthy social boundaries.
14. Unsafe people are unstable over time, rather than proving to be consistent and dependable.

Think for a moment about yourself, your inner child, your tendencies, your issues, and your vulnerabilities. In view of these things that you know about yourself, look back over the fourteen traits above, and attempt to *pick the five* that would potentially be the most harmful to you.

Circle the numbers of those five unsafe characteristics, and omit (cross out) the names of any candidates who seem to have as many as four of them most of the time. (Don't be too hard on your people! Nobody is perfect, and it is very hard to find really good candidates. Sometimes a person will have some strengths or redeeming qualities that will justify tolerating his or her weaknesses. In such cases, simply be aware and cautious!)

Application

To conclude this chapter, give thoughtful and prayerful consideration to the candidates who have survived the final screening and still remain on your list. Remember my earlier comment that it is best to have at least four or five different people on your final list.

List your finalists below and how you might go about getting their agreement to be one of the "other caring people" in your support system as you complete your reparenting:

_____

_____

_____

_____

It is now up to you to follow through in allowing some special, caring people, and one or two special, caring groups or organizations, to be vital, helpful links in the chain. One, two, three … *go*!

Little Mona Did It

I can vouch for the importance of "other caring people" in the process of reparenting, but I can also appreciate the tips and cautions given in this chapter. Little Mona did not have the benefit of that information, and neither did she have the list of characteristics that help identify "unsafe people." She had to learn a lot of this the hard way, and her lessons began very early in her life. The result was severe and repeated abuses that led to many years of physical, emotional, and mental turmoil.

Mona eventually learned to spot unsafe people pretty quickly, like the man who sat down next to her at a social event and kept wanting to talk about her feet. She simply excused herself and moved to a different table.

I didn't see it coming, though, when a minister visited me on a cold January day several years ago. My mother was in the hospital on a respirator at the time, and he came to my apartment to express his concern. I invited him in, and we sat on the couch and talked. All that needs to be said here is that he made some sexual advances, I resisted, and he finally left. The effect on me, however, was devastating. My old, confusing, self-condemning self-talk started up again. I believed it must have been my fault, that I must have given out signals somehow, and that I must be a horrible person. I felt that my body was evil and that it must be punished. I swore that it would never feel anything anymore, and soon my eating disorder started up again. My faith suffered greatly and almost collapsed. It was a long time before I would trust anyone, and I don't know what would have happened if God had not sent several safe, caring people across my path.

Using a blend of professional counseling and biblical principles, Dr. G. offered me the best of both worlds! Through this kind of guidance and unconditional, positive regard, my faith was restored, and I began very slowly to risk trusting some other caring people.

I began attending services at the Wholeness Community. Some of them included meals. I decided to attend for awhile to learn more about what they did. I didn't know that I would begin to appreciate this unique ministry and that I would later find there a place of leadership and service.

I had found a new church, where I got to know Pastor Sergio and his wife, Beth. I had started crying during a closing prayer and didn't think anyone had noticed. The next day, though, they called and asked if I was OK. On a Wednesday night, Beth noticed that I had written a poem, and she asked if she could read it. It was about how I used to think that God was like men I had known in my life and how I learned He was so different. She read it and said, "I felt just that way several years ago myself." She asked me if I would meet her for lunch. I did and found out that she was a beautiful person on the inside as well as on the outside! As our relationship grew, she became a great blessing and an instrument of healing for me.

The time came when I had to face the fact that I was anorexic. I did that through Dr. Colin Ross's Fern Meadows Trauma Program. The staff and the patients there touched my heart on a deep level. Sometimes we joked and broke the tension for each other. One staff person there who gained my trust and respect was Joan Smith, an intelligent, sensitive, but firm lady. Others who helped me greatly were Dr. Bernard Gotway and Dr. Fontaine, who became my psychiatrist on the outside. I also want to thank Carrie, Phyllis, and all the trauma staff for helping me regain my empowerment.

When I returned to church, I found that Pastor Sergio and his wife (my friend), Beth, were leaving to do mission work in Mexico. My abandonment issue began to kick in, and I grieved the loss of their friendship. At the same time, I was having serious dental problems that were often very painful. I did not have insurance or finances to cover the dental work. I felt alone, discouraged, abandoned, and afraid.

Then a friend brought Brother Jim to talk to me about my dental problems. Before long, I had a real appointment with a real dentist, who attended Brother Jim's church. Through six months of dental surgery, I developed trust and confidence in Dr. Hallmark and his assistant, Angela. I became a good patient and eventually walked away with a good set of dentures and a brand-new smile!

A few months later, Dr. Gilliam said we had achieved our treatment goals, and after seven years, he released me from therapy. Walking out the door, I realized that I did it! Yet I knew that I did not and could not have done it alone. I thought of all the people past and present who had helped me, who believed in me.

I thought of all the patients whose stories and struggles had touched me and inspired me. I thought of all the people who donated money to help me with the dentistry. I thought of all the people who prayed for me and with me. I thought of Sue, who reached out to me with warm sensitivity when I was so alone. I thought of how all my alters helped me to survive the abuse and have now integrated to make me a whole person again. I thought of God, my heavenly Father, who had all this planned before the beginning of time. To God and all these people, I give my deepest gratitude and love. You are the safe and caring "other people" without whom I could not have completed my reparenting! I am so glad that I took the risk of allowing you into my life!

Chapter 19

Planning the Role That "God, Your Father" Must Play in Completing Your Process of Reparenting

Vantage Point

ONE OF OUR seminars is entitled "Intimacy with God, Your Deepest Human Longing!" Some people have objected to this title, claiming that it sounds too sexual to refer to a relationship between God and a human being. Such an objection reveals that the objector does not understand the difference between sex and intimacy. People can certainly have intimacy without sex, and (unfortunately) it is also possible to have sex without intimacy. Of course, it is possible (fortunately) to experience both simultaneously.

In the seminar, we study the many facets of His Godness and how it would change our lives if we were to allow each facet to become a reality in our personal relationship with God. In case this all sounds too ethereal and mysterious for you, feel free to skip the next two paragraphs.

In Scripture, God uses several different names to refer to Himself, and each name has a meaning that progressively reveals additional facets or aspects of His Divine Personhood. For example, the first one mentioned (*Elohim* in Genesis 1:1) means "The Creator" or "Omnipotent Power over the Universe," but it does not reveal a personal trait to which we can relate. Later references, however, reveal His capacity for significant, caring intimacy, such as, "The Lord is my Shepherd" (*Ra-ah* in Psalm 23:1), which may also be interpreted as friend or companion. Finally, both Jesus and Paul address Him directly as "Abba," an Aramaic word for father, which almost parallels the personal intimacy of our use of the words "Daddy" or "Papa." (See Mark 14:36; Romans 8:15; Galatians 4:6.)

The fascinating fact is that each facet represents a point of potential connection between His personality and ours, providing us with multiple possibilities for interface and intimacy. According to 2 Peter 1:3–4, these become opportunities for us to become "partakers of His divine nature," which includes and makes available additional *intimate qualities of parenting,* such as healer, provider, protector, comforter, source of peace, and others. More information of this nature is easily found, but one source that has been especially inspirational to me is Kay Arthur's book entitled *Lord, I Want to Know You: A Devotional Study on the Names of God,* published by Waterbrook Press.

The important application for this chapter is the need to understand and accept the fact that the meanings of God's names reveal facets of His Godness that represent intimate parenting qualities that are available only from Him and that are necessary to complete your process of reparenting.

That's what this chapter is about.

Input from Dr. G.

Back in Chapter 16, there was a good bit of discussion about the extreme importance and tremendous impact of your self-image. Whatever image you project to yourself, inside yourself, and about yourself, all your mental faculties will "gang up" and work together to help you (or make you) measure up (or down) to match (and continue to match) that image.

Several paragraphs (including a chart) were dedicated to the three factors that determine this image and the problems that often emerge when those factors are deficit or unavailable. Also included in that chapter were the profound principles that follow:

1. Each of the three factors comes more from one particular significant other than from anyone (or everyone) else.
    *   That sentence may sound a little confusing, but it is actually rather simple in its application. It is simply referring to the fact that *usually and traditionally*:
    *   Your sense of *belongingness* comes more from your *dad* (or a father figure) than from any other individual.
    *   Your sense of *competence* comes more from your *mom* (or a mother figure) than from any other individual.
    *   Your sense of *self-worth* comes more from *someone other than you mom or dad,* who is very important to you! This *someone* is often an actual big brother, but it does not have to be. This *someone* can be almost anyone who crosses your path and becomes significant at a crucial point of readiness. The point is, this person *will* leave an indelible impression that either validates or invalidates your sense of *self-worth.*
2. Nobody had perfect parents, nobody is a perfect parent, and nobody was a perfect child; therefore, *everyone reaches adulthood with certain deficits in his or her self-image factors.*
3. If/since your primary caretakers failed to provide all the positive input and role-modeling that you needed, *you can depend on the Lord to intervene and provide remedially in two ways:*

First, He will bring across your path individuals who will possess personal qualities and characteristics that will correct or complete the work that your primary caretakers were supposed to accomplish in your self-image.

Second, God Himself will personally complete the work, if you will let Him. In other words, there is a final touch that only God can provide to correct your self-image and complete your reparenting. And each Person of the Godhead (Trinity) will perform the specific role for which He is uniquely equipped, as follows:

- The heavenly Father will correct your father-deficit and complete your sense of *belongingness*.
- The Holy Spirit will correct your mother-deficit and complete your sense of *competence*.
- Jesus Christ, the Son, will correct your "Big Brother" deficit and complete your sense of *self-worth*.

Not every reader will be interested in knowing this much detail about the specific dynamics God has chosen to apply, but some of you will be intrigued and fascinated with the transcending tri-unity of the Divine design He has crafted and choreographed to provide healing, wholeness, and completion to your reparenting.

Taking It Personally

To make this very personal, please look up each of these Scripture references, and fill in the blanks to indicate what God is offering or promising to do for you:

Example: Psalm 27:10: He promises to be with us, even if our own father and mother forsake us.

- Deuteronomy 31:6: He promises to go with us and that He will not _____ us or _____ us.

- Hebrews 13:5: He promises never to _____ us or _____ us.

- Matthew 6:9: We are allowed to think of Him as "our _____."

- Psalm 34:18: He promises to be near us when we have a broken _____.

- Psalm 86:15: He is described as a God full of _____, _____, _____ , _____, and _____, which He offers to all His children.

- 1 Peter 5:7: We are assured that we may cast our _____ on Him because He _____ for us.

- Isaiah 40:11: We are assured that He will feed His flock like a _____, that He will _____ the lambs with His arm, that He will _____ them in His bosom, and that He will gently _____ those who are with young.

The twenty-third Psalm begins, "The Lord is my ; I shall not want." That Psalm continues through all six verses to list many blessings and benefits of being a member of that flock and belonging to that particular Shepherd. List a few of those blessings and benefits in the space below:

_____

_____

_____

_____

The last two verses of that Psalm make it clear that the Psalmist is not just talking about an actual Shepherd and literal sheep. For example, you do not usually set a table for sheep or pour them a cupful of beverage. This becomes even clearer as the Psalmist concludes with the words, "… and I will dwell in the house of the Lord forever." Somewhere along the way, the sheep of that Shepherd translated into the children of a great, eternal household that is referred to in the final verse as "the house of the Lord."

Take a moment, close your eyes, and imagine yourself as one of the children in that great household, enjoying all of the blessing and benefits listed above.

There is one more point of really good news for you to add at this time. Here it is, and I would like for you to read it aloud now. Ready, go: "I do not have to wait until some future time to start enjoying all of this. All of it is available to me right now. Thank you, Lord."

Transitional Point: Notice *that just as with an earthly father, there are some benefits that a son or daughter of the heavenly Father may receive simply because they are the Father's children. The children do not have to earn these benefits or perform tasks to receive them. The only condition necessary to receive these benefits is to be the Father's child(ren). The last two Scripture references above present this idea and reveal some of the benefits. An additional passage of Scripture that states this idea clearly is Romans 8:16-17, which follows: "The Spirit itself bears witness with our spirit* *that we are the children of God: and if children, then heirs; heirs of God, and joint-heirs with Christ; if so be that we suffer with him, that we may be also glorified together"* (italics mine).

Finally, consider Galatians 4:7 as confirmation of this transitional point: "Wherefore, thou art no more a servant, but a son; and if a son, then an heir of God through Christ."

I realize that a paragraph that begins with the word, "Finally," should not be followed by another paragraph! Consider this as a postscript or an addendum, if you wish, but it just seemed necessary to make two things clear before moving on: (1) Not everyone is presently a child of God and, therefore, does not qualify for the blessings and benefits referred to above. (2) Anyone can become a child of God by meeting the conditions expressed in the following verses: "As many as received Him [Jesus], to them gave He the power to become the sons of God, even to them that believe on His name" (John 1:12). "That if thou shall confess with your mouth the Lord Jesus, and believe in your heart that God has raised Him from the dead, you shall be saved; for with the heart man believes unto righteousness, but with the mouth, confession is made unto salvation" (Romans 10:9–10).

Application

Having just made the Transitional Point above, I must now seemingly contradict myself by pointing out some exceptions. This is not really a contradiction but an additional way in which God's role in completing your reparenting is like an earthly father's role in parenting his earthly sons or daughters.

Just as we have pointed out that there are some blessings and benefits that sons and daughters receive simply because they are the offspring of their biological parents, there are also some potential blessing and benefits that have some conditions attached to them. It is not unusual for a biological parent to make a privilege or reward contingent upon completing a chore or task assigned by the parent. There may be an allowance, for example, that a child receives just because he or she was born into the family and reached a certain age; but other benefits, perks, or permissions may definitely be conditional, and the requirements may be defined by the parent(s).

Give a few other examples of blessings or benefits to which a parent may often attach some conditions, i.e., "You can do or have this *if* you do (or stop doing) that!"

_____

_____

_____

_____

God, as the ultimate parent, has also chosen to make some of His blessings and benefits conditional. Look up the verses that follow and list the benefits and the conditions He has set for receiving them:

- 2 Corinthians 6:17–18

  Benefit(s) _____

  Condition(s)_____

- Isaiah 26:3–4

  Benefit(s) _____

  Condition(s)_____

- Philippians 4:6–7

  Benefit(s) _____

  Condition(s)_____

- Philippians 4:8–9

  Benefit(s) _____

  Condition(s)_____

- Isaiah 40:31

  Benefit(s) _____

  Condition(s)_____

- 2 Chronicles 7:14

  Benefit(s) _____

  Condition(s)_____

- Psalm 1:1

  Benefit(s) _____

  Condition(s)_____

- Psalm 37:3

  Benefit(s) _____

  Condition(s)_____

- Psalm 37:4

  Benefit(s) _____

  Condition(s)_____

- Psalm 37:25

  Benefit(s) _____

  Condition(s)_____

- Psalm 37:34

  Benefit(s) _____

  Condition(s)_____

- Psalm 37:38–39

  Benefit(s) _____

  Condition(s)_____

- Proverbs 3:5–6

  Benefit(s) _____

  Condition(s)_____

Now, please look back over the benefits you just wrote down in this exercise. Obviously, they are all great, wonderful, and desirable blessings, but please *put check marks* beside six or seven of the ones that seem most vital, most important, and most necessary to you.

From the benefits that you checked, select your top five priorities, and list them below:

- Benefit No. 1— _____

- Benefit No. 2— _____

- Benefit No. 3— _____

- Benefit No. 4— _____

- Benefit No. 5— _____

These benefits and blessings are likely the ones on which you should focus in order to allow God, your heavenly Father, to do His part in completing your process of reparenting.

So, what does this look like, and how do I get it to happen?

The answer is: You meet the conditions associated with the five benefits you listed above. And as the benefits begin to emerge in you, they filter to your child within, who receives "the blessing" in much the same way that Hebrew fathers used to pass "the blessing" to their sons and daughters in Old Testament times. (See Genesis 31:55; 49:28; etc.)

So, list below the condition(s) associated with the five benefits you listed above. (You may list more than one condition on the same line, if more than one relates to the same benefit.)

- Condition(s) No. 1— _____

- Condition(s) No. 2— _____

- Condition(s) No. 3— _____

- Condition(s) No. 4— _____

- Condition(s) No. 5— _____

After you have written down the relevant conditions, look them over, think about them, and write out your thoughts as prompted below:

Which of the conditions will probably be the easiest for you to meet?

_____

Which of the conditions will probably be the hardest for you to meet?

_____

What kind of strategy or preparation will you need in order to get started?

_____

Who would be a good person (or two) to hold you accountable?

_____

If you cannot take on all of the above conditions at the same time, place a check mark (above) beside the ones you will start working on first.

Set a date and time when you will seriously start working on meeting these conditions:

_____

You have come a long way on your reparenting journey. Do you understand that these conditions are crucial in allowing God to perform His role in completing that process? With this in mind, how strong is your commitment on a scale of 1 to 10 (with 10 being the strongest)? _____ If it is below 9, read Philippians 4:13, and ask someone to pray for you.

The time has now come for you to be prayerfully thoughtful and thoughtfully prayerful! *Use the space between the questions below to write some notes, phrases, and sentences that will help you organize your thoughts so you can pray the prayer you need to pray in a few moments.* Your prayer will need to be serious, intelligent, effectual, fervent, and on target. Although Jesus will interpret your prayer to the Father, it would be best for you to pray a grown-up prayer rather than a kindergarten prayer at this time (Rom. 8:26-27,34; James 5:16).

Note: The purpose of this prayer is to ask God to assume His role in completing your process of reparenting. To accomplish this, you should also request His power and blessing (1) upon you to meet the conditions successfully and (2) upon your inner child to experience healing, wholeness, and intimacy with the Father.

How will you start it off?

_____

_____

_____

Do you need to start with praise and/or thanksgiving?

_____

_____

_____

Do you need to confess anything to "clear the air?"

_____

_____

_____

What are the benefits and blessings you are seeking?

_____

_____

_____

How can you express the intimate, fatherly relationship you need with Him?

_____

_____

_____

How can you tell Him what you want Him to do for your inner child?

_____

_____

_____

What problems might you face in meeting the conditions?

_____

_____

_____

What kind of help do you need from the Lord?

_____

_____

_____

What specific requests do you need to make? (Review the purpose above.)

_____

_____

_____

Are there any promises or commitments you need to make to Him?

_____

_____

_____

Is there anything else you need to pray about while you have His ear?

_____

_____

_____

How shall you close, and in whose name shall you pray?

_____

_____

_____

Now it is time to pray. You can probably verbalize your prayer by looking at the notes and comments that you wrote above. If you need to write it out in narrative form, please use another sheet of paper, and staple it to this page in your workbook after you have prayed.

When you have finished praying, write a brief report below on how you felt during and after your prayer.

_____

_____

_____

_____

Little Mona Did It

I will admit that I delayed doing this chapter because it was the hardest one for me to do. My real father died when I was a month old, and most of the men I've known, both as a child and as an adult, have been abusive. So I had a really hard time with the idea that God could be like a father to me. To Little Mona, that meant either He wouldn't be there or He would be abusive. To me, the adult, it seemed that He was so holy and perfect that I could never be good enough to qualify for His fatherness.

Then God showed me Isaiah 43:25, where it says that He chooses not to remember all the times I blew it but will think about my desire to please Him and be His daughter. Then I thought of my own daughter and that I no longer focus on the number of dirty diapers I changed when she was an infant. Instead, I think today of the joy, the love, and the laughter we shared. Suddenly, I seemed to "get it," and I was ready to tackle Chapter 19.

We are taught in this chapter that there is a final touch that only God can provide to correct your self-image and complete your reparenting. We are told that He is willing and able to do this, but He usually goes about it in a special way for those of us who didn't get very good fathering as children.

In other words, for those of us with pretty big father deficits, He will often start by bringing certain people across our paths who can serve as father figures and somehow model or show us what fathering is supposed to be like. It could be a coach, a grandfather, a neighbor, a Sunday School teacher, or almost anyone else who shows up at the right time, with the right qualities. Or it could be several different people. I would like to tell you one of the ways God went about filling such a vacuum in my life.

Several things had gone wrong in my family and in my life in general. There was a lot of conflict; my mother was getting sicker; and I was feeling a lot of stress, anxiety, and fear. During one sleepless night, I decided what I would do the next morning. I called my new pastor, and he met me at a nearby McDonald's. We sat and talked about my mother's illness and other conflicts in my life. We talked about the anger and rage that had surfaced. I told him about my Dissociative Identity Disorder (D.I.D). I Asked him if he knew of any counselors that could help me. He told me about Dr. Larry Gilliam at Dayspring Counseling and gave me his phone number.

Here are the thoughts that went through my mind: *Dr. Gilliam? Three doctor's degrees and almost thirty years experience? A man who just wrote a book? He probably would not want to see me. He probably doesn't take my insurance anyway. My daughter's in foster care, I'm on Social Security, all my relationships have failed, and I've lost every job I've ever had. He may not be that impressed with my stunning accomplishments!*

I got up the courage to call him. It was his cell phone, and he answered it personally. He sounded gentle, courteous, and kind. We set an appointment time. I was still expecting to be rejected when he met me in person.

I showed up at the appointment. He had three offices, but this one was in a church facility in Irving. I was beginning to feel frantic because I couldn't find an unlocked entrance, and I knew being late would not be a very good first impression. I was almost crying because I was trying so hard not to be late. I tried door after door.

Finally, I went around to the back, and there was this older gentleman getting out of his car. He asked if he could help me. I said, yes, that I was trying to find a Dr. Gilliam. He smiled and said, "Well, you just did! Come on in!" We both laughed, he unlocked the door, and we entered the building.

I had not drawn any conclusions on the phone about what he would be like in person. He seemed very relaxed and casual. He seemed professional but very easy to talk to. He didn't even mention my insurance!

I can't really recall what we talked about at this first session. He gave me a workbook he had written and told me not to do it all in one sitting, which had been my plan. After the session, he asked me if I would like to come back. I said that I would.

I didn't know I was starting a seven-year journey that would lead me to healing and wholeness. I did know that I had been accepted and invited back! That caused me to suspect that there may be some hope after all!

Things were not always pleasant between us. We worked hard and long, and sometimes we pushed each other to our limits; but I kept coming back each Friday, and he kept on seeing me! At times, when alters would come out angrily, harshly, or in an accusing or threatening manner, we would find a way to resolve the conflict, reconcile, and get back to work.

Dr. G. would not let me get by with believing that my true identity was "victim," that I was inherently a bad person who deserved to be abused, or that I was worthless and unlovable. He refused to stop believing in me and continued to offer me hope and safety.

The point for now is that I saw in him certain qualities that I somehow knew were reflections of how fathering ought to be. Finally, I realized that if I could see some of these traits in a mere human being, then how much greater must be the possibilities of relating to the Fatherness of God!

I think this set the stage for God, the Father, to perform His role in my reparenting.

Chapter 20

Preparing a Program of Maintenance and Follow-up to Retain and Reinforce the Benefits of Reparenting

Vantage Point

CONGRATULATIONS! YOUR PATIENCE and perseverance are about to pay off. As a bystander once said when a toddler's diaper fell down around his ankles, "The end is in sight!" It is the end of the workbook that is in sight, however, and not the end of your learning, your growing, or your need for maintenance and follow-up. That is the reason why doctors, lawyers, and certain other professionals refer to their work as their "practice," because there is always the next thing to increase their knowledge, broaden their experience, and sharpen their skills. That is the kind of thinking that will help you retain and reinforce the benefits of your reparenting.

According to your Process Checklist, you have almost completed thirty steps spread throughout twenty chapters. You have endured the emotional roller coaster rides, survived the mental "flips and zooms," and overcome the inherent and inevitable game of "chutes and ladders," which may suddenly slide you backward a chapter or two and require you to re-climb (or reclaim) a stretch of the road you have already traveled! Your achievement is outstanding and noteworthy, as you have truly and successfully turned a "millstone" into a "milestone!" (That one was for the adult. Get it?) If I were in your presence right now, I would pitch you a chicken nugget! (The Kid will immediately appreciate this symbolic gesture!)

There are a couple of things I can actually offer, however, that should help us emotionally mark and appropriately celebrate your achievement. One is a personalized document that welcomes you into the Society of Childlike Persons, with all of the rights and privileges appertaining thereto. The other is a Certificate of Completion signed by me and the Chairman of our Board, confirming that you have successfully completed both volumes of the Reparenting Course. This is certifiable through the Dayspring Institute for Training & Development.

If you would like to accept this offer, call the Dayspring Counseling Services in Irving, Texas, after you have finished this workbook, and leave your contact information with the receptionist. The present number is 972-570-9828. If that number has changed when you call, try information for the new number, or get updated contact info from our website at www. dayspringcounseling.org.

Input from Dr. G.

There is something I need to tell you at this point, and I hope you will accept it at face value. Here it is: *Because you have traveled (and travailed) a significant distance, and because you have ingested and digested two volumes worth of material and experience, you will never be the same. You will never again be exactly as you were, and that is a good thing. Maybe you have seen the bumper sticker that says, "I'm not what I ought to be, but Thank God, I'm not what I used to be!"*

Do you remember the analogy we used back in Volume 1, that once you have dug a hole, you can never pack all of the dirt back into it like it was before? We concluded that it is almost as hard as trying to unsay a word after it has been spoken and heard, which prompted this little limerick:

> I would think it a trifle absurd
> To attempt to unsay a word;
> And it's similarly clear
> That no functional ear
> Can unhear what it's already heard!

Or you may think of the reparenting process like the birth of a baby in this respect: once the delivery (or deliverance) has begun and reached a certain point, it is not likely to reverse itself.

It was probably in the eighth grade, maybe the ninth, when I had to memorize "The Chambered Nautilus," a poem written by Oliver Wendell Holmes in 1858. The meaning somewhat impressed me then, but I find it very interesting that it comes back to mind after half a century as I search for the best way to illustrate a major point.

The chambered nautilus is a snail-like sea creature with a spiral shell consisting of many chambers, each larger than the one before it. In nature, the creature starts with a single shell; but as it grows, it builds a larger chamber to move into, and it seals off the chamber it has outgrown. As this continues throughout the creature's life, the original shell becomes a spiral of many chambers, each larger than the one before.

Verse three of the poem describes this process as follows:

Year after year beheld the silent toil
That spread his lustrous coil,
Still, as the spiral grew,
He left the past year's dwelling for the new,
Stole with soft steps its shining archway through,
Built up its idle door,
Stretched in his last-found home, and knew the old no more.

Our point is that the little creature can never move backward into a chamber that he has outgrown and sealed off. First, because he just would not fit there anymore. Second, because God gave him instinctual wisdom to seal off that part of his past. He truly has moved on.

There's an old, southern, colloquial expression that is used sometimes when a person realizes that his only viable option is to keep moving. In this old saying, the person is apparently quoting a rabbit in the field who has heard the barking of some pursuing hounds. The grammar of this statement may be questionable, but the truth and wisdom of it cannot be denied: *"I done jumped up, and now I gotta run!"*

Once you have breathed some mountain air, smelled some freedom, tasted a little independence, and felt a little relief, your heart will reach for more release. This is your innate, God-given quest for life that stretches you beyond your bondage of the past and hungers to be more than a survivor! If this is where you are in your journey, then you will be touched by the challenge in the final verse of the Nautilus poem:

Build thee more stately mansions, O my soul,
As the swift seasons roll!
Leave thy low-vaulted past!
Let each new temple, nobler than the last,
Shut thee from heaven with a dome more vast,
Till thou at length are free,
Leaving thine outgrown shell by life's unresting sea!

It is no longer necessary for you to back into the future focused on a painful past. Like the prophet Isaiah, you can "set your face like a flint" and walk into the future with confidence and hope (Isaiah 50:7)!

Taking It Personally

In a nutshell, here is what I am recommending for your maintenance and follow up. A wise man once said, "If you would be pungent, be brief; for words like sunbeams, pierce deepest when concentrated." So I will keep it compact and to the point, as best I can.

I have chosen one more time to use an acrostic, so you will have easy recall and some "nails to hang your thoughts on!" (I just noticed that if you spell acrostic with two *S*s, it has even more significance for this occasion, i.e., A-CROSS-TIC! Never mind.)

M—Maintain an awareness of your inner child.
That part of you will be with you all your life, and you don't want to lose the healthy ground that you have painstakingly gained.

A—Assure and re-assure the child in ways that calm his or her fears.
Remember that many issues are fear-based, and each of the primal fears needs a certain kind of re-assurance to calm and counteract it.

I—Interact with and pray for the child.
Use the effective ways you learned to communicate with the child as you continue your quest to become more childlike and less childish.

N—Nurture and nourish yourself physically, emotionally, and spiritually.
This translates into taking good care of yourself. Remember: the best parenting thing you can give the child is a healthy adult counterpart.

T—Take a searching and fearless inventory of your belief system yearly.
Situations and circumstances can infect your belief system. Make it a point to clean the filter and recalibrate at least once a year.

A—Allow other safe people and support groups to be a part of your life.
Yes, this will be a hassle, but iron still sharpens iron. It is healthier than the alternative, and you may end up blessing someone else.

I—Improve your skills in Basic Life Management, including "choices."
There are three domains to manage and budget: money, time, and energy (physical and emotional). Review the chapter on making choices.

N—Never stop learning and growing!
I have known some people who stopped and stagnated. Their minds and souls shriveled up, and they became bitter, lonely, old people.

In this case, follow-up is the simple matter of continuing to maintain.

Application

Long ago, early in my many years of graduate school, I was asked to compose and present a socio-drama, incorporating certain principles of psychoanalytic theory. While I do not wish to endorse that theory, there are two songs I wrote as a part of that forty-five minute, pre-recorded presentation that seem strangely appropriate for bringing this chapter (and this workbook) to a close.

The first is entitled "The Song of the Ego," and it was sung by the character representing the practical side of a person. This character was dressed as a vaudeville performer, with hat and cane in hand, and he sang the following words to the tune of "There's No Business Like Show Business" (Curtain, please):

> Be prac-tical, in-fac-ticle, exac-tically real!
> Never does a mere hallucination,
> Aid digestion or assimilation,
> Remember to subject each inclination
> To scientific investigation!
> Your mere insistence won't change existence
> No matter how strongly you feel!
> Tho' your ideality may have its place,
> It is reality we must face,
> And in actuality we must embrace
> That which we taste, see, and feel! (Oh, yeah!)
> That with which we can deal! (Uh-huh!)
> That which makes up a meal! (Ya got to!)
> That which really is real!

Hold your applause! I just wanted to say that there is an element of truth in this little song that I would like to leave with you. Did you get it? Do you see it? What is something about these lyrics that might be a good message to teach the next generation? Please respond below.

_____

_____

_____

_____

The other song is entitled "The Song of the Super-ego," and it was sung by the character representing the moral and ethical side of a person. This character was dressed in a dark robe and had a halo mounted above his head. He entered majestically and sang the following words to the tune of "Somewhere Over the Rainbow":

> Keep your morals and values, way up high!
>> Look yourself in the eye
>> And give life an honest try.
> Keep an ear to your conscience, live thereby
>> Hitch your life to a star,
>> You're more than you think you are!
> But if you tumble from your star
> And stumble to my judgment bar
>> I'll find you!
> And if you let reality
> Infect your personality
>> I'll still remind you!

Keep your eye to the sky, look way up high!
You can start where you are, and climb for another star!

I haven't thought of these lyrics in ages and had to think hard to remember some of them. But honestly, I almost entertained a tear or two as I recalled the meaning and the heart of the message and realized the depth of my desire that you, the reader, will catch it and receive it and apply it.

Last, but not least, I would like to close with something I did not compose but could easily wish I had. It is free-verse, and I first heard it back when the earth's crust was still warm! No, not that far back, but way back when television used to sign off at midnight. Yes, there was a time when T.V. stations would shut down at midnight, and lots of people would actually go to sleep!

Back in those days (or nights), the stations would usually sign off with a touching thought or song and, finally, with the National Anthem. Often, where I grew up, the presentation before the National Anthem would be this touching free-verse reading about the soaring, transcendent feeling of freedom and release that a certain pilot would experience as he "flung his craft through footless halls of air …"

During a counseling session a few years ago, some of the words came back to me, and I quoted them to a lady who needed encouragement. She was deeply touched, went and found the words, and had a calligrapher pen them and frame them. That gracious gift is now mounted on my office wall.

At times, I used to read it on my radio program, and I usually choked up a little toward the end. I share it with you now as the icing on this many-layered cake.

High Flight

By Lt. John Gillespie Magee, Jr.
Oh, I have slipped the surly bonds of earth
And danced the skies on laughter-silvered wings;
Sunward I've climbed, and joined the tumbling mirth
Of sun-split clouds … and done a hundred things
You have not dreamed of … wheeled and soared and swung
High in the sunlit silence. Hov'ring there,
I've chased the shouting wind along, and flung
My eager craft through footless halls of air.
Up, up the long, delirious, burning blue
I've topped the windswept heights with easy grace
Where never lark, or even eagle flew.
And, while with silent, lifting mind I've trod
The high untrespassed sanctity of space
Put out my hand, and touched the face of God.

May you ascend to similar spiritual heights as you experience
His promises in Isaiah 40:31 and Psalm 16:11.

Little Mona Did It

Yes, Little Mona really did it! She struggled her way through each step of each chapter a little ways ahead of you, and we have tried to share what that journey was like for us, in hopes that you would be encouraged to continue through the harder parts yourself; and here you are! You have made it and are literally only moments away from the finish line!

There are some mixed emotions as we put together our segment of this final chapter, because it is the last thing you will read, and it will leave some kind of taste in your mouth. It needs to be good and helpful and bring the workbook to some appropriate close.

It also needs to be real and personal. So, here is our decision: we will close by sharing the final five steps of how we got from diagnosed Dissociative Identity Disorder to the healing and wholeness that we enjoy today.

First, I had to assert myself and come to grips with my D.I.D. I had to take my stand and state my own understanding of who I was and who I could become. Here is the poem I wrote as my Declaration of Independence to some of the medical and mental health community:

We Will Take Acceptance

Every time I talk to you, you act like you know what is inside.
You have your own take on my life, that's why I withdraw and hide.
I feel like you sit in judgment, like you know all about D.I.D.
Because you sat in class and studied! Well, you haven't studied me!
I have people who have specialized, studying and practicing many years,
But I know my "system" better than anyone—their hopes, dreams, and fears.
We all want understanding and acceptance: we're not stupid, evil, or insane,
If you really knew this disorder, it's a defense to cope with severe pain!
Please be patient with us, we cope with life the best we know.
It hurts to be misunderstood, yet I try not to let it show:
"We are the walking, wounded children."

Second, Little Mona had to be recognized and accepted. Here is the poem I wrote to change her identity from "Nobody" to "Little Mona."

Mona

I have renamed you "Mona," even though it once brought us shame.
"Nobody" no longer fits you; please have the joy of having a name.
You are somebody special, a priceless gift beyond measure,
A unique, valuable person, the apple of God's eye, a treasure!
"Nobody" is now "Mona"—a fetus that has worth!
I will help you become strong, you will make it to birth!
You are much more than a mass of tissue, soon a newborn baby,
To grow and reach your potential: doctor, lawyer, president, maybe!
I will be your nurturing mother, to guide, protect, and give you care,
Welcome to life and the family! Little Mona, so innocent and fair!

Third, I had to renew and redefine my relationship with God. At the same time, this also freed me from the bondage of perfectionism. You can see how those two issues are related in my next poem.

I Don't Have to Be Perfect

I don't have to be perfect, because I have been forgiven.
Having perfection as a goal makes life not worth livin'.
I don't have to be perfect, God loves me warts and all,
He's always there beside me, in the morning and when evening falls.
I don't have to be perfect, I can reach to overcome and excel,
To be true to His name, and to wisely live and tell.
I don't have to be perfect, I will strive to give my best,
I'll strive to keep making progress, and my sins on Him to rest.
I don't have to be perfect, just love and have compassion,
To live up to my potential, to follow my dreams and passions.
I don't have to be perfect, I can make mistakes and still be loved,
Because now I understand: imperfection is what this life is made of.

Fourth, I had to make a great exchange. I had to make the huge decision to trade in the victim role for a life as a real person, namely me! I like to think of that as a major change of clothing, and I expressed that change like this:

The Great Exchange

Tonight, I turned my victim rags into a princess gown!
They saw it as a celebration, I got a freedom's crown!
Tonight I put my foot down, on verbal and physical abuse,
On pushing, shoving and cursing—I can be put to better use.
I say "Yes" to life, I deserve happiness, too!
I'm not who they think anymore—I got better things to do!
I say "Yes" to God, I believe this is His will,
I say "No" to continual hurt, I am a person who is real.
I say "Yes" to myself, to be all that I can be,
From nobody to somebody—at long last, I am me!

Finally, I had to continue my counseling with perseverance, over a long period of time. I have now graduated from my therapy, but many, many Fridays, I rode the bus for hours to keep my appointments with Dr. G. Sometimes sessions went well, and other times they felt more like something that rhymes with "well!" We hung in there, though, and as it says in the title of my little book, *We D.I.D. It!* Here is my final emotional marker, which includes a heartfelt word of appreciation to Dr. G.:

Yours Truly, Office

When I go to see you on Fridays, I never want to leave.
I want to grab hold like a child, because when I go I grieve.
I don't know why you believe in me, when the years don't support that fact.
I expect your anger and rage, but next Friday I'll be back!
I acted out of fear at times, it wasn't at you I was screaming,
You told me what happened while I slept, confusion, terror, and dreaming.
You always seemed to understand me, being a sheltering rock of sorts,
In times of high winds and storms, giving wise counsel and gentle support.
I just want to thank you, may God always richly bless!
I believe in you too, Dr. G.—you are one of God's best!

In closing, I will leave you with a comparison of the old rules I used to live by and the new ones that now characterize my life … most of the time!

Some of the rules I used to live by that no longer apply to my life are:

1. Don't feel or talk about feelings.
2. Be good, right, perfect, and strong at all times.
3. Don't be who I am, because that's not good enough.
4. Don't ever make others angry or uncomfortable, or they will leave.
5. Do what others want you to, even if it hurts.
6. Always be funny, but don't enjoy life.
7. Don't trust my decisions, other people, or even God.
8. Trust untrustworthy people, and then feel hurt when they let me down.
9. It's wrong to ask directly for what I need or want.
10. Don't get very close to anyone; it isn't safe.
11. Don't grow or change, because it makes other people uncomfortable.
12. Don't succeed because it makes other people feel inferior.

Some new rules that now govern my life are:

1. It's OK to feel feelings and to talk about some of them to safe people.
2. I can make some good decisions and solve some of my own problems.
3. I do not have to be perfect all the time to be OK.

4. I am OK as I am, but I can get better as I grow and change.
5. It's OK for me to succeed, even if it makes someone unhappy.
6. I can make mistakes, admit them, and forgive myself.
7. It's OK to make human errors and to have a bad day at times.
8. I can do some things very well, and occasionally, I can be great!
9. I can get better at recognizing safe people and unsafe people.
10. I can say "no" to people, and they can also say "no" to me.
11. It's OK for me to take care of myself and to nurture myself.
12. It's OK for me to have fun and to enjoy life.
13. I can usually trust myself, and I can always trust God.
14. I can allow myself to get close to safe people who earn my trust.
15. I can be vulnerable enough to risk developing some true friendships.
16. I can love and be loved and have a more intimate relationship with God.
17. These new rules are helping me become a healthier, happier person.

It has been an honor to have a part in your reparenting. Always remember this: "If Little Mona did it, then you can do it, too!" And with God's help, you can.

(NOTE: Ramona Russum is dedicated to leading groups and otherwise offering help and hope to others. Her book, *We D.I.D. It!* and her collection of poems are published by Lone Star Productions of Dallas, Texas.)

Conclusion

IT WAS STATED in the foreword that Volume 1 of the *Reparenting* workbook is sort of pre-op. It is necessary preparation that gets you ready for the heavier experience. In other words, if your total experience of reparenting took only one week, your completion of Volume 1 would probably put you somewhere during the afternoon on Wednesday.

It was further stated that such an achievement should be cause for rejoicing and motivation, not for despair and withdrawal. Wednesday is sometimes called "hump-day," because it is the middle of the week, you've got some momentum going for you, and the farther into Wednesday you go, the surer you feel that you can make the rest of the week!

Congratulations are in order because you accepted the challenge, rose to the occasion, and somehow persevered through the rest of the week! It is also noteworthy that, in many ways, the second half of that week is harder than the first half! In Volume 2 the incision is deeper, the therapy is more intense, and (I'm sure you noticed) the workbook is considerably thicker. The good news is that you hung in there. As the old saying goes, "You rode that horse all the way into the barn!"

While there are many benefits and rewards for your achievement in terms of health, wholeness, restoration, and recovery, I would like to provide a couple more that you probably did not expect. I would like to offer you, at no cost, the following acknowledgments:

1. A Certificate of Completion from the Dayspring Institute for Training & Development—signed by me and the Chairman of the Board.
2. A Certificate of Membership in "The Society of Childlike Persons"—a rather precious, personalized, and frameable document entitling you to collect rainbows, smell flowers,

talk with animals, hold hands, and enjoy numerous other activities that delight childlike people of all ages and set them apart from grumpy, old grouches!

You may request these free documents, if you wish. Write a letter, stating that you have completed both volumes of the Reparenting Workbook, include a brief testimony of your experience, and mail it to Dr. Larry Gilliam, Dayspring Counseling, 3317 Finley Rd. Suite 168, Irving, TX 75062. Or email dayspring.counseling@yahoo.com.

Appendix

"ABUNDANT" AS DEFINED in the *World Book Dictionary:* "More than enough; very plentiful; full supply; rich; abounding." <"The Lord…[is] abundant in goodness and truth" (Exodus 34:6)>

SELECTED SCRIPTURE REFERENCES REVEALING SOME FACETS OF THE ABUNDANT LIFE*

- **God wants us to have abundant lives.** "…I am come that they might have life, and that they might have it more abundantly" (John 10:10b).

- **God is able to provide such abundance.** "Now unto Him that is able to do exceeding abundantly above all that we ask or think, according to the power that worketh in us…" (Ephesians 3:20).

- **God is willing to provide such abundance.** "Wherein God, willing more abundantly to shew unto the heirs of promise the immutability of His counsel, confirmed it by an oath…" (Hebrews 6:17).

- **Such abundance is centered in and funneled through Jesus Christ.** "…for your furtherance and joy of faith; that your rejoicing may be more abundant in Jesus Christ…" (Philippians 1:25b-26a).

- **God's most basic provision of abundance is salvation.** "…For so an entrance shall be ministered unto you abundantly into the everlasting kingdom of our Lord and Saviour Jesus Christ" (2 Peter 1:11).

*see page 154

SELECTED SCRIPTURE REFERENCES REVEALING
MORE REGARDING ABUNDANCE

- Exodus 1:7 -- Abundant increase
- Psalm 36:8 – Abundantly satisfied
- Psalm 37:11 – Abundance of peace
- Psalm 72:7 – Abundance of peace
- Psalm 132:15 – Abundant blessing
- Isaiah 35:2 – Abundant rejoicing
- Isaiah 55:7 – Abundant pardon
- Isaiah 66:11 – Abundance of glory
- Jeremiah 33:6 – Abundance of glory
- Zechariah 14:14 – Abundant wealth from the heathen (eventually)
- Matthew 13:12 – Abundant spiritual understanding
- Matthew 25:29 – More abundant talents
- Romans 5:17 – Abundance **of grace**
- 1 Corinthians 12:23-24 – Abundant honor and comeliness
- 2 Corinthians 1:12 – Abundant wisdom and grace
- 2 Corinthians 4:15 – Abundance of grace
- 2 Corinthians 7:15 – Abundance of affection
- 2 Corinthians 8:2 – Abundance of joy
- 2 Corinthians 9:12 – Abundant thanksgiving
- 2 Corinthians 11:23 – Abundance in labors
- 2 Corinthians 12:7 – Abundant revelations
- Philippians 1:25-26 – Abundant joy and faith
- Titus 3:6 – Abundance of the Holy Spirit
- 1 Peter 1:3 – Abundant mercy
- 2 Peter 1:11-Abundant ministries

Selected Bibliography

Arno, Richard G. *Temperament Theory*, Tenth Ed. Sarasota, FL: National Christian Counselors Association, 1992.

Arno, Richard G., and Phyllis J. *Creation Therapy*. Sarasota, FL: National Christian Counselors Association, 1993.

Asper, Kathrin. *The Inner Child in Dreams*. Boston: Shambhala Publications, 1992.

Bennett, Rita. *Making Peace with Your Inner Child*. Grand Rapids: Fleming H. Revell, 1992.

Dickenson, Richard W., and Carole G. Page. *The Child in Each of Us*. Wheaton, IL: Victor Books, 1995.

Hemfeld, Robert, Frank Minirth, and Paul Meier. *Love Is A Choice*. Nashville: Thomas Nelson, 1989.

LaCour, Jean M. *Counseling the Codependent: A Christian Perspective Utilizing Temperament*. Sarasota, FL: National Christian Counselors Association, 1996.

LaHaye, Tim. *Spirit Controlled Temperament*. Wheaton: Tyndale House, 1966.

LaHaye, Tim. *Your Temperament: Discover Its Potential*. Wheaton: Tyndale House, 1984.

Leman, Kevin, and Randy Carlson. *Unlocking the Secrets of Your Childhood Memories*. Nashville: Thomas Nelson, 1989.

McGee, Robert S. *The Search for Significance*. Nashville: Thomas Nelson, 1998.

Minirth, Frank. *Happiness is a Choice Workbook*. Richardson, TX: Frank B. Minirth, 2012.

Minirth, Frank. *The Power of Choice: The Normal Zone Workbook*. Richardson, TX: Frank B. Minirth, 2012.

Missildine, Hugh W. *Your Inner Child of the Past*. New York: Simon and Schuster, 1961.

Seamands, David A. *Putting Away Childish Things*. Wheaton: Victor Books, 1993.

Warren, Rick. *The Purpose Driven Life*. Grand Rapids, Michigan: Zondervan, 2002.

Contact Information

To order additional copies of this book, please visit
www.redemption-press.com.
Also available on Amazon.com and BarnesandNoble.com
Or by calling toll free 1-844-2REDEEM.